The Conversion

by David Jezierski

CREDITS

Copy Editor:
Mary Walsh

Proofreaders:
Julie Geary
Fr. Joseph Marcotte
Anita Compagnone

Book Cover Designer:
Ken Vaudrain

Printed by
Kerrin Graphics & Printing, Inc.
42 West Dudley Road
Dudley, Massachusetts 01571

DAVID
860-336-7305

CONTENTS

Book 1
Raised in the Faith and Still Went Astray

Chapters

Book 2
Married Life and Human Weaknesses

Chapters

Book 3
Saved from Eternal Punishment and Religious Concepts

Chapters

Book 4
Called to Imitate Christ Through the Church

Chapters

Book 5
The Interior Writings

Preface

All of the names in this book have been changed. I have used biblical names in place of real names. I want to protect the identity of the individuals out of respect to them. There might be things in this book that you don't agree with, but I wrote them as I perceived them. I personally have high expectations of certain individuals in the Church and their responsibilities to the Church.

Many of us don't truly understand the power of conversion and the effects on the person's life after experiencing a conversion. It's a life-changing event that takes an individual from who they once were to someone they know nothing about. It erases part of their past memories and often leaves them in a confused state. It creates a new desire to search for the One who saved them. It also allows them to look at their past and realize that they would have perished for all eternity. It opens their blind eyes to see past what they couldn't see before. They leave the world they once loved in search of the lover who freed them from their imprisonment. Still held back by some of the chains of their sinful ways, they struggle to free themselves, with God's grace, in the hope of drawing closer to Him. Torn between two worlds, they must choose one. They realize they cannot live in both and be truly happy. Not knowing what lies ahead of them, they put their faith in something that cannot be felt by human hands or seen by the human eye. They learn to breathe and survive through an interior love that comes and goes at will. They feel blessed and cursed as they try to continue forward through the rejection and persecution of those around them. They find new friends and start a new life in Christ, leaving much behind them as they continue on a new path and new journey through the unknowns ahead of them. Every person that walks the face of the earth is on a journey. The belief or non-belief in God is your own personal battle and your journey. The only guarantee in life is that it will come to an end whether you're prepared, or not. I have found that there are those who think they understand God and His ways—who in their thinking have become blinded by their decisions, still unable to see the truth. I was one of them. My decisions in life moved me further from God, even when I thought I knew Him. The sad reality is that many of us go through life thinking and believing that we know Him. We really don't. When we were young, we failed to see ourselves traveling through time, growing older and closer to the end of our life here on this earth. We engaged in all kinds of social events without seeing ourselves falling away from God.

This conversion is a true story, a personal journey away from God and my return to Him. It is my hope that when you read this story you will relate to the struggles in your own personal life. It is also my goal that you see past your blindness and limitations, for all of us are somewhat blinded to our own selves and are limited by our blindness. This book tells about my childhood, when I was innocent and naïve, and the lessons my parents taught me in life that were taken from me through an act of violence. It continues with me, as a child, trying to survive in a world physically, while struggling to find love. As a child, I was torn between the principles of good and evil, thinking that good only brought me suffering. Feeling abandoned by God, I decided to choose a world of sin, finding pleasure in it and continuing a journey deeper into a sinful lifestyle. As a teenager, I perceived love in sexual relationships and continued that journey towards the fantasies and lies in them. As an adult, I was transformed from an ugly duckling to a somewhat good-looking man. Overwhelmed by the change, I became full of self-love and pride and journeyed further into sin and further from God. In an act of desperation, I cried out to Him and He heard me.

In the conversion, I talk about my struggles with certain concepts of religious thinking. I also talk about my struggles through the conversion, trying to find God in a deeper way, struggling to become a better Christian, and battling with past memories of my sinful ways. As I journey deeper into the Church I fall in love with, I'm awakened by the corruption within it. Relying on God's love as my strength, I journey through a world of rejection in the hope of one day being with my one true love.

Book 1

Raised in the Faith and Still Went Astray

1

Only God Can Save Us We Are Unable to Save Ourselves

The power of a true conversion is to know that God saved the soul from being lost because the soul existed in a world of darkness. He allowed His light to penetrate the soul creating the desire to move towards the light. It is through the love and mercy of God that this can happen. The person must have complete understanding that on their own they are unable to change their path. It was God alone and nothing the person did or deserved. We must also understand that even the worst of sinners can achieve the impossible through Jesus Christ, our Lord and Savior, and that all can be saved and live in the joy of the light.

We know that Jesus Christ did not come for the healthy, but for the sick. I walked among the sick and I was getting sicker by the day because of sin. In time, I would have perished into the world of darkness for all eternity. Because of the prayers of many and the love and mercy of Jesus Christ, I experienced the power of a true conversion. I will no longer walk among the dead. I have a new hope knowing that someday I might be walking through the doors of Heaven: a new home of true peace forever immersed in the love of God. This is my conversion story.

It has been eleven years since my conversion which happened on my wife's birthday in the year 2007 at a Protestant church. I would like to share with you some of the events leading up to my conversion, and some after my conversion: from my first experience with God as a child, through my sinful years before my conversion, and finally through some of my beautiful experiences after my conversion.

Raised in the Catholic Faith

I was born into a Catholic family. My parents were and still are devout Catholics. Even today my mother reads religious books in hopes of drawing closer to our Lord as we all are called to do. My father still tries to attend Mass every day and to remain faithful to God through that route. Both of my parents try to watch daily Mass and many other devotionals on the Catholic channel and to develop a powerful prayer life. I know in my heart that my parents tried to the best of their ability to raise us in our Catholic faith. What might have made it difficult for them to raise us in the Catholic faith was that they were raising us during Vatican II. Let me explain: my parents were raised in the era when the Church taught about fire, brimstone, and the punishment of Hell. People were taught about sinning and how it offended God. They took sin very seriously. When Vatican II arrived, it moved the Church away from the punishment of God to the love and mercy of God through Jesus Christ. My mother at first struggled with this transition, but over time moved on and accepted this renewed emphasis of the Church. I think my father adapted well because he believes everyone's going to Heaven and no one's going to Hell. The Church teaches accountability: we are all accountable for our actions and the sins we commit against God. I have had several discussions with my parents on this subject. My father always tells me that nobody ever came back to tell us about Heaven or Hell, so based on the information we do have, it will be up to each and every individual to make their own decision. This isn't Church teaching, but he's entitled to his own opinion.

As a child I did not grasp what our parents were trying to teach us about our faith. I believe many religions struggle reaching young people, not just the Catholic Church, but all churches. As a young boy I was taught a lot of rules without understanding the depth and purpose of them. I struggled with trying to understand the Catholic faith but even though I struggled, I somehow was able to embrace the love of both God and my parents. My parents tried very hard to teach us about our faith and also the importance of prayer and how to pray. I am saddened to say that I have very little memory of what we were taught about our faith: not because my parents failed to teach us, but because of my lack of interest back then.

I have four other brothers and three remain faithful to the Faith: my older brother Noah, my twin brother Philip, and my younger brother Joseph. My brother Stephen, who is the second oldest, chose to be an atheist. His decision broke my parent's hearts. My parents have offered up many prayers and sacrifices for his conversion back to God and they continue and will continue making sacrifices for his soul until the day they die. In recent discussions with my brother Stephen, he has told me that he has tried talking to God but has received no response. I felt that way, myself, at times prior to my conversion. It's an emptiness we all feel when we think God is not responding. But are we truly asking? Are our hearts and minds really open to hear Him within us? Eventually I followed in my brother Steven's footsteps and fell away from the Church and away from God.

Childhood Life

Our parents raised all five boys to attend church every Sunday and tried to instill in us the need for Church and God. I can honestly say our family was close when we were younger; it wasn't until we entered the teenage years that we began to fight. I was the most aggressive and fought with Stephen often. We had a void when we didn't get along and I hold myself responsible for that. We were all wild and drove fast and recklessly except for my brother Joseph. My poor father and mother had so much to worry about, words cannot describe the headaches and heartaches we caused our parents with our driving and sassy mouths. I believe their prayers and their faith in God carried them through all the hardships they had to endure.

We are close today and try to help each other out as much as possible. When we were younger, we did a lot of things together and had some good times. We did a lot of things outside like playing baseball, basketball, and football: we did the things all boys did. We were a handful for my mother and father and they loved us all the same. We were disciplined when necessary and always felt loved because my parents knew how to love. They sacrificed much for us and continue sacrificing for us even today. I fail to love as my parents love. I lack the capacity in my soul to truly love others as I should, though my mind understands the concept of what love is. I have much to learn and am open to learning. I pray someday that I can love as my parents love.

What I do remember is when I was a young boy I had a paper route in Massachusetts. I had an old rusty bike which I left at my grandmother's house who resided in Massachusetts. I had a couple of paper routes which provided me with a little bit of money so I could buy candy at the local store down the hill from us and my father put the rest of my money in the bank for me. One of the routes I would do with my brother Philip during the week on a Wednesday afternoon. The other paper route we did as a family on Sunday mornings with our father who drove us around. I only used the bike that was left at my grandmother's house to do my paper route on Wednesday afternoons.

First Intimacy with God

I remember one sunny afternoon at my grandmother's house I had a great urge to spray paint on my bike fenders and all over my bike the words "Jesus" and "God." I was around the age of nine or ten. I went into my grandmother's basement to get my bike and a can of black spray paint that was lying around in the basement. I went outside and spray painted my bike as best I could. I remember the joy I felt in my heart on that day while I was doing this. It was a joy that is hard to describe: possibly an inner peace and a feeling of being loved, truly loved, as if God flooded my heart and soul with His immense love. I do not think I have felt that kind of interior love again—almost thirty-five years later. There is a joy that you get from the Holy Spirit that is different from the joy that you get from the things of this world. It was not the joy that you might experience when you buy something for yourself that you always wanted, but something different. It was an interior joy; not something that would come from something external, but something internal. It was different than all the other joys I have ever felt in my life. Those who have experienced this joy will understand what I am talking about.

Love of God Taken from Me Through an Act of Violence

I remember that when I would take my bike out for a ride, I felt invincible. There was something powerful in those words that were written all over my bike. I felt like I was on top of the world as if I were surrounded by a power that could not be touched. I was so proud of my bike when I was riding it, but soon that would come to an end. One day I was delivering papers on my Wednesday afternoon paper route with my brother Philip who rode down another street to deliver papers. A young girl, in her late teens to early twenties, came out of nowhere while I was standing next to my bike and pushed me down to the ground. She jumped on top of me, held me down, and threatened me. She demanded I give her all of my money. I was just an innocent boy who had never experienced violence or the pain it caused. So I gave her my paper route money and she ran away. I looked at my bike that was lying on the ground next to my feet, then I looked up at the sky. I remember crying, feeling crushed, and no longer feeling invincible. I felt betrayed as if God had not been there to protect me from the evil this girl had just inflicted upon me. I remember the look in her eyes as if I were looking into an empty temple that contained no feelings or emotions. An empty vessel that was being filled through my suffering and her dubious accomplishment. She never turned back. She seemed unable to feel any remorse. I began to compare us. She was strong and I was weak. She was without fear and I was terrified. She was damaged and I was broken. Her life appeared to be empty and my life was full. My household knew love and her household knew war. We were worlds apart and yet God loved us both.

I am not sure if on that day I lost all hope in God. My heart was broken, I felt abandoned and betrayed by God who was my everything. And my perception of people changed as well. I was a child who only knew love and always felt loved. For the first time in my life, I was unable to see love in everyone. Evil found its way into my heart and planted its roots deep within my soul. I think I felt anger towards people for the first time in my life, something deeper, something sinful that I had never felt before. From that day on I just wasn't the same. The happy boy I was died on that day. My heart had a taste of hate and my mind understood this creature of evil.

Later in my teen years my father best described my problem when he said to me in the gentle loving way that was his nature, "Why are you carrying this chip on your shoulder?" My mother, who was the firm one she had to be, was also very loving. The Lord blessed me with great parents and no one can take that away from me. I thank God now for blessing me with great parents. Back then I was too young to know better and I am glad the Lord woke me up before it was too late.

The Move to Connecticut and the Sacrifices of My Parents

I attended a Catholic school in Massachusetts all the way up to the completion of fourth grade when we moved to Connecticut. My parents decided to buy some property in Connecticut because the house they owned in Massachusetts was too small for our family. My brothers and I had to share bedrooms and beds because of the lack of rooms inside the house. My father worked two jobs to support us and somehow was able to put a little money away for a down payment on a property with a large gravel pit in Connecticut. Back then the property was considered a risk to purchase and develop, but my father was determined, and was eventually able to develop the property. People also weren't interested in waterfront property, making it inexpensive to purchase—not like it is today. My parents were considered by others to be frugal with their money, which they did in order to send us to Catholic schools. When my parents were in need of money for our education, they sold hundreds of yards of gravel to the state of Connecticut which was used to help build a major local highway. They even sold some of their property to send us to Catholic high schools, but kept some property in the hope of their children building their houses there someday, which we all did. What hurts me the most is that some of my father's fellow workers thought he had money, and every so often would jeer him, and call him cheap. Yes, we had a house on a lake, technically known as a pond on the map. Also, back then, my parents' status would've been considered, at best, middle-class. I think back about how some people treated my parents because they thought they had money. What little they knew. My parents never went anywhere, never took a vacation, or attended anything that would've cost them money so that we could receive a good Catholic education. Those people weren't there to see all the sacrifices my parents made; all they saw was what they wanted to see. I want you to know that, while my parents' friends and fellow employees were enjoying the good life, my parents were living the sacrificial life. Believe me, my parents knew poverty well: they knew how to go without and how to sacrifice while managing what little money they had. Yes, it looked like we had money, but the truth is my parents struggled and went without so much for the love of their children. The reality is, people will believe what they want to believe regardless of the facts.

When we moved to Connecticut, I'm not sure if I continued playing baseball in Massachusetts for another year or two but I know I did not play baseball in Connecticut as a child. From fifth grade through eighth grade I attended another Catholic school in Connecticut. I had had a great time at the Catholic school in Massachusetts, so it was a little bit of an adjustment to attend the new school because I didn't have many friends. I felt like a loner and I'm not sure if it was because of our moving to Connecticut, or my still being upset or troubled about being robbed which I believe happened at about the same time. I can never be sure if this was the cause of my feeling some anger inside myself, but it definitely was a life-changing event that I believe was the start of my anger problems. That anger would continue to grow inside of me all the way up to my conversion. Don't get me wrong: I still had laughter and joy in my life with family and friends, but part of me walked around still an angry child. It would not be until I entered high school that the sin of anger would begin to compound and build inside me to the point of rage.

Catholic Schooling

Our parents always had concerns about our well-being and sent us to Catholic schools. All of my brothers and I attended Catholic schools from kindergarten to the completion of high school. When it was time for me to attend high school, my parents sent me, along with three of my brothers, to a high school in Connecticut. My oldest brother Noah finished his high school in a different Catholic high school and my second oldest brother Stephen had to finish his last two years at the same high school I attended because the Catholic high school he was attending closed. My youngest brother Joseph and my brother Philip, who I've been close to most of my life, also attended the same high school I attended.

In our freshman year my brother Philip adapted better than I did, but was still limited to hanging out with the students whose parents were on the same financial footing as my parents. Like most schools, students tend to separate themselves into groups based on financial status. Unfortunately, the more affluent separated themselves from the rest of us. I wish they had realized that money doesn't determine the person, rather the person is determined from within. There is so much we could learn from each other if we would only give the other person a chance. Who knows what hidden treasure might be found in another individual. I became friends with three other individuals like myself. Unfortunately, they did not stay the whole year because of the peer pressure that certain students put on them. As I think back, a sadness fills my soul because my friends deep down inside had beautiful hearts and were sensitive individuals. In the world of the rich, the poor tend to be frowned upon because the rich fail to look at the individual for who they are instead of what they possess. Some students never gave us the opportunity to show them who we really were. We were judged by our appearances which did not fit the standards of the other students. I have to admit we were different: longer hair, maybe some acne—just cosmetic stuff. The clothes we wore were what our parents could afford. We tried to fit in as best we could, but were unable to. My friends came from parents who didn't have much money either and most of the other students came from families who were well-off. Soon my friends left the school one-by-one and I remained there alone without any friends to laugh and share stories with. I was the last of the outcasts: I was feeling the pain of being alone and I was angry.

Part of me is glad today that my parents kept me there; I feel if they did not I would have been worse off than I was. Unfortunately, I failed my first year, and was forced to retake some classes. I wanted to go to a different school with some friends I met over the summer of that year. They had a summer cottage or knew someone that owned the cottage that was on the same lake I lived on. We became close friends—they were always in trouble and soon I got into trouble with them. My parents never knew the things we did when I stayed at their house; I never said much to them when I got home. On occasion we would break into their neighbor's barn and steal their beat-up motorcycle and ride around the neighborhood with it. My new friends also influenced me to smoke cigarettes and do mischievous things. At the time, it appeared to me to be the normal thing to do; I was losing awareness of right and wrong. Slowly the devil was pulling me away from God and the truth. He was holding my hand, gently tugging on it, leaving me unaware of his presence as we walked together deeper into the world of sin.

Unable to Embrace Bad Love

I remember having feelings for my friend's sister and she felt the same way towards me, but I was too shy to ever ask her out. I felt ugly in appearance because of my skin's complexion and the way I took care of my hair, and my clothing was not stylish. She came from the same world in appearance but not financially or through her upbringing. I never saw our common ground and believe to this day that God protected me from what would have been a disastrous life. She probably would have ended up pregnant because I was too weak to resist the temptations of my sinful desires. I probably would have been forced to marry her because it would have been "the right thing to do." The backgrounds that we possessed in morals and principles would never have sustained a marriage and would have ended in a divorce. The reason I think this is that there was no foundation to build on through God's love. Her father drank all the time and was an alcoholic. He was a heavy smoker with very few principles or values. Her way of thinking was very similar to her father's—she had little or no faith and also poor work ethics. I was too naïve to understand or to know any better about these things that my parents knew much about. I remember on several occasions arguing with my mother because I thought she was being too snotty, and I did not hesitate to tell her she was too snotty. Later in my life I realized she was not the person I thought she was, she was the mom who was watching out for me. At that time I thought my mother was looking down at my new friends because we had a house on the lake and went to private schools. I know now my mother was trying to protect me, which a good parent would do for love of her children.

Bad Influences Causes Much Suffering

I was strongly influenced by my friends and their lifestyle and decided that I wanted to change the high school I was attending to attend my friend's public school. I remember arguing with my mother on several occasions, but she would not yield. It did not matter what I said to my mother, there was no way she was going to take me out of my Catholic high school and put me into a public school. My insults never broke her and she held to her conviction. My parents were always watching out for my best interests and decided against sending me to the high school I wanted to go to. Because of their decision, I would have to learn how to survive in a high school where I did not want to be. It was challenging for me to remain there in an environment with kids who were well-off and spoiled, who looked at me as an outcast. I felt like a fish out of water. It was an environment that I knew nothing about.

I am in tears thinking about the sacrifices my parents made for us. How they wanted the very best for us and gave what little they had to us. I remember my mother making some of our clothes and my father working two jobs to make ends meet so that we would have some kind of future. I wonder how such love and devotion produced such a sinful child? Why is a child blinded in his youth to such great love? Why do we search for so many places to fit in and feel wanted? The beauty of God is that he can take anyone, no matter how bad they are, and turn them into something so beautiful and precious.

By my junior year, I would have such anger and hatred towards my fellow classmates that I would constantly be in fights. Eventually I became feared by most of my classmates and teachers. I was out of control and I didn't really care. I had a rebellious and violent attitude with little or no fear of anyone. At that time in my life, I was not happy with my parents' decision to keep me at that high school. And because I was miserable, I made it a point to make everybody else's life miserable.

The problem with some students and parents is that they tend to elevate themselves above others because they possess more or feel they are better than others. How we perceive success could be our biggest downfall. Success should never be measured by what you possess or how great you think you are. Success should be measured by your ability to love. You do not need wealth or power to love, because love comes from something greater than that. It is a free gift given to us from above—a gift which we are all encouraged to share with one another. The source of love is God who created all things out of this love. There is nothing in this world that can trump love.

10

Worlds Apart

I did some dating later in my junior and senior years with very little success because of my appearance and how I dressed. I remember asking a girl from my high school to go to a semiformal with me and she turned me down. I remember having strong feelings towards her but was too stupid to realize we were worlds apart. I had nothing—in the sense of materialism—and she had everything. I think, in the depth of my heart, even if I were a different person she would not have looked past our worlds. I lived in a world of wanting, she lived in a world that had everything. Though I was ignorant to the understanding of love, something deep within me believed in it. I never dated any of the girls from my high school, probably because I was not too appealing to anyone and had bad acne along with a bad attitude. I dated some girls outside of my high school who attended public schools. As a whole, I did not really date too much and my relationships did not last long. I found myself dating girls whose lives were troubled just like the life I was living was troubled. I did attend some proms and live the high school life as best I could. There really is not much to reflect about on this subject.

The one thing I remember the most in high school was when I was in class studying psychology. On this particular day, the teacher was not there so a substitute teacher filled in. While I was in class, the substitute had to leave for moment, and when he left the room, one of the students grabbed my book from me to challenge me. Other students joined in. I was outnumbered and they decided to throw my book out of the classroom window which was on the second floor. I had no fear or was just too stupid to realize what I was about to do. So I looked out of the window, then back at the classroom, and jumped. I landed into some bushes below. As a result of the fall, I fractured my ankle and felt a slight discomfort but was too proud to notice it. Or maybe I did not really care because I was full of anger and hate; I'm not quite sure. The classroom below us at that period in time was a Spanish class. I found out later that some of the students in the Spanish class were looking out of the window when I jumped. I am not sure if they were looking at the time or if they were laughing or just in shock when they saw me falling before their eyes into the bushes. As I was standing up trying to get out of the bushes, the substitute teacher came running out of the building, pulled me out of the bushes, and muscled me straight to the headmaster's office. I remember looking into his eyes when he pulled me out of the bushes. They were full of anger and disgust. And at the same moment in time, I think he was trying to figure me out. I think in his mind he was wondering why I did such a stupid thing. The substitute was a big guy like his brother who had been a professional football player at one time. I probably felt like a paperweight to him because I only weighed 99 pounds. It wasn't long before I was in the office in front of the headmaster awaiting punishment. The sad reality is that when your heart is full of anger, it is also feeling the emptiness from rejection. I was not born to hate; I was just a victim taught to hate through the actions of others. The world they lived in never understood the world I lived in and we were never able to meet in the middle. We remained worlds apart.

11

A Troubled Teenager

Now the school had a lot of leaves to rake and we had a rake day for that reason. On Rake Day all the students got together and would have to rake up all the leaves on the school campus. My punishment was to rake leaves for a week straight. My parents were disappointed and upset with me and I could not blame them for feeling that way. There were several reasons why my parents felt the way they did, primarily that I continued to bring shame to our family's name through my attitude and my actions. I could not blame them for feeling the way they did because they deserved better than I gave them. I was the troubled child with the bad attitude and I could not seem to control myself or my anger. It was hard on my parents. My parents did everything they could to try to change my direction, but when your soul is filled with evil you need a miracle.

All my life, before my conversion, I never had the desire to read a book and I found them boring as well as challenging. Even while I was attending school, I somehow got away with never reading one. When I was in high school, I always relied on other classmates to help me with my school subjects. I was good at prying information out of them whether through fear or because they didn't want to be seen with me. Whatever the reason, I got away with it and ended up graduating with my classmates—the ones I started high school with in the ninth grade. To this day I'm amazed that I graduated in four years. I think that the priests and teachers all wanted me out of their school and I really can't blame them. I was always getting into trouble and had no respect for teachers. I had a reputation of fighting in the hallways of the school and was known for inflicting fear because of my personality. They had to consider what would be in the best interest of all of their students. I ended up graduating second from the bottom of the class which brought shame to my parents. I was blinded to the suffering I caused my parents who deserved a better son. I did not know love, only hate. My parent's love was not enough; I needed more and was unable to find it. Hate found its way into my heart and became my only friend while love was outside the door of my heart trying to get in.

I graduated from my high school with no fond memories and no high school friends. It was a tough four years with a lot of rejection and only regrets. When I think of the stories my friends used to tell me about their high school I wonder how it could have been if I were different. I often think of the high school I attended and how it has changed so much since I attended school there. In my opinion it used to be a good Catholic high school run by priests. Now the school is run by the laity and is becoming more and more secular and drifting away from the origin of truth.

While I was still in high school and living at home, my anger was building up because I was dealing with the rejection of classmates and feeling alone.

I was spiraling into darkness. My mother, being a very prayerful person and a member of a prayer group, decided to have some of her prayer group come down to pray over me. At first I rebelled, but later gave in. I'm not sure if it was because I got tired of my mother's asking me, or if I just wanted to put an end to this foolishness. I felt embarrassed about people praying over me like I was a special needs child. I don't quite remember why I allowed them to pray over me, but I did finally allow it. At first I felt stupid, surrounded by what I thought back then was a group of religious fanatics. I have to admit, though, that when they were praying over me I felt an inner peace that calmed my spirit. It is hard to describe, but the anger was gone from me and I felt at peace. My mother was so happy for me and the prayer group praised the Lord for His love and mercy. They felt confident that I was healed and I would be okay. There was only one problem. After you are delivered from the evil that dwells within you, you have to change direction. You cannot continue with the same lifestyle because it will be just a matter of time before you become your former self. My environment remained the same—I had no prayer life and nothing to sustain me, so I continued with my lifestyle and became my former self again.

Forgive me if I go back-and-forth in time. I sometimes feel that something might have to be inserted as I try to explain things. I remember how angry I felt because my life appeared empty to me. I had no friends and, even though I had a good upbringing, it wasn't enough to fill the void in my empty heart. My father tried to reach out to me on several occasions, but was unable to. I was just an angry and rebellious teenager with a bad attitude. I remember on one occasion fighting with my mother when I was home with her while my father was at work. I was very angry and believe I slammed the front door when I left in a fit of rage. My mother immediately locked the door behind me, out of fear, then kept the door locked in hopes of calming me down. All I can remember is I was outside at the front door screaming at my mother to let me in. My mother was standing inside the house refusing to let me in until I calmed down. I kept screaming at her to let me in and my mother kept telling me to calm down. She refused to unlock the door in an attempt to keep me out of the house. I remained outside the door looking in at my mother and I was full of rage. The hate inside me was burning like a fire out of control. In my mind, I was thinking there was no one who was going to keep me out of the house. I remember throwing my fist through the glass window of the door, reaching in, unlocking it, and walking into the house without a care in the world. I looked into my mother's eyes without remorse. I had become just like the person who robbed me years ago. We were both formed by the evil that enters us and then consumes us. Our sins were different and yet had the same effect—causing someone else undeserving pain. After looking her in the eyes, I proceeded to walk by her, staring at her as if I were king, letting her know I would never be stopped—I was too strong for her. I was a proud and foolish teenager who caused my parents a lot of pain and suffering they didn't deserve. My past brings tears to my eyes as I remember the pain and suffering that I caused many. I am not proud of the things I did and never will be. I feel compelled to share this with you so you will understand the power of my conversion. I am laying down a foundation so you will understand who I was.

I also remember on several occasions kicking holes in the interior doors of my parents' house when I had my fits of rage. I found it hard, if not impossible, to control the rage and anger I felt inside me. As a result of my anger, the doors inside the house needed to be repaired. My father was handy and my mother insisted that the doors be repaired. They were shameful reminders to a mother who refused to see the bad in her children whose only desire was to see good in them. Eventually my father put in wooden grills to repair the holes of the kicked in doors. The wooden grills still remain on the doors today. My painful reminder of my sinful past.

Another time I was mouthing off to my mother and feeling totally out of control. My mother, in desperation, had to call my oldest brother, Noah, out of his bedroom where I believe he was studying. My brother came out of his room unhappy with me because I was arguing with my mother again. He looked at me, then around the room and saw a piece of lumber—I think it was a 2 x 4. He picked up the wood and looked at me. I looked back at him and seeing his anger, I turned and ran into the bedroom as he chased me. I stood by my bedroom window, cornered with nowhere to go. When we looked each other in the eyes, my eyes were full of fear and my brother's full of anger. I was trapped and felt I had no choice but to jump out of the bedroom window to escape. I opened the window and jumped out to the ground below, then ran away into the woods across the street from our house. My brother remained in the house—I'm not sure why. I don't know if my mother told him to let me go so I could be left alone, but, whatever the reason, I felt safe for a little while. Miraculously, I survived the jump of about ten feet without injury.

Physical Injuries Resulting from Pride

As a result of jumping out of windows and doing stupid things, I ended up fracturing my ankle several times. I am not sure of when or how many times, but I have been examined by doctors and asked how I fractured them. I could never give a specific time or place because I kept reinjuring them. There were times in the past when my ankles troubled me a lot especially when I played softball. Both of my ankles have bone spurs as a result of the abuse I put them through. One specialist said that I had bone spurs as a result of fracturing them so often and the abuse I put them through playing softball. We discussed surgery but he felt it was too risky because I could end up with limited use of my ankles, so I decided against surgery and I just live with them.

On one occasion a few years back, I had to change doctors due to new insurance. I remember having my first visit with a nurse practitioner for my physical. I remember her checking my ankles and her shock because of their flexibility. She wanted a second opinion, so she asked my permission to have another doctor look at them. A part of me was laughing inside because of the look on her face and her concerns. I gave her permission and she left the room to get the doctor. They both came back into the room, the doctor introduced herself, and proceeded to examine my ankles. As she was examining my ankles, she looked at the nurse practitioner, concerned, then looked at me and asked how long they been like that. I explained to the both of them how my ankles were fractured many times and how flexible they are and may have been that way for many years. They told me they had never seen ankles that bend like mine.

My Parents' Desperation

It finally got to the point that I was so out of control that my parents, in desperation, put me in their car and drove me off to drop me off at a seminary somewhere in Massachusetts with hopes that a priest could straighten me out. Believe me, my parents loved me but they were out of options and running out of hope. My parents got out of the car and, while I sat in the car waiting, walked towards the building and were greeted by a priest. The conversation was brief and they returned to the car disappointed. Unfortunately for my parents, the seminary was closing the following year and was not accepting any more students. My parents were at a standstill and got into the car. As we were driving home, I remember the disappointment in my parents voices as they were talking to each other while I sat in the backseat, gloating over some victory that I thought I had won. They were hoping the seminary could have saved me or at least reformed my thinking. The Lord knew I did not belong there and yet we drove there to that particular seminary. Out of all the possibilities, why there? I also know the seminary would have been wrong to accept me even if they were not closing because I believe being a priest is a special calling and no one should enter the priesthood for the wrong reasons. In the past, the Catholic Church has suffered much because men have entered the priesthood for the wrong reasons. It was a great disappointment for my parents and yet the Lord allowed it. Did my parents fail to discern God's will which we all must do otherwise we cause ourselves unnecessary suffering? Unfortunately for my parents, it got to the point that there was no talking to me. My parents put their hope in the seminary and not God which resulted in heartache. This happens to everyone who does not try to discern what God wants for them or when they put their hope in something else besides God. In their hearts, my parents felt their last hope fading away as we drove towards home.

14

Entering the Working World

Somehow I made it through the high school years and now it was time to go out and work in the world. I did have a part-time job in high school working at a gas station to pay for my car and gas, but now it was time to get a real job.

My twin brother also worked at the same gas station while we were in high school. We were inseparable. We eventually got our first real job together at a shoe factory in Massachusetts: I worked on ejection molding machines that made soles for shoes and my brother Philip worked in expediting. It was a factory environment and I adjusted to the environment quite nicely. The use of foul language was right up my alley—men and women. Also, the men in the factory perceived women as sexual objects. This attitude was not helping my soul. Their desires to fulfill their sexual fantasies through perverse conversation was fueling my inner desires, creating a false illusion of women. As men, we were not looking at the beauty of a woman's interior, which is part of her personality, but we were looking at them for sexual purposes only. We perceived them as sexual objects because they walked around in loose clothing and had foul mouths—both men and women without morals and principles dwelling in pools of perversion and lust. Sin ran rampant and our souls continued to plunge into darkness. Fortunately, not everyone succumbed to the evil within that place because they were older and wiser and had a stronger foundation within them. Unfortunately, most of us were too young and spiritually weak, building a house upon a foundation of sin.

15

Attending High School as a Postgraduate

Eventually my mother felt that my brother Philip and I were going nowhere in life, working at a shoe factory with no future. She persuaded both of us to quit our jobs and work part-time while attending a trade school as postgraduates. I often think how my brother Philip and I were close most of our lives. It was only after we went to trade school and completed our courses that we would eventually go our separate ways. We attended a trade school in Massachusetts. I studied electrical and my brother Philip studied plumbing. It was difficult for me, who already graduated from high school, to go back to school with high school kids. I was not a mature adult and had anger issues. The worst thing for me at that time was to be surrounded by high school kids because they made me less mature. It was like being in high school all over again but, instead of battling the wealthy students, I had to battle students of a different nature. The students I hung around with now were very immature and pranksters. I remember a girl in the trade school that I thought was cute. I told one of my friends how I felt about her, and on Valentine's Day my friends decided to send her a Valentine's card with my name on it. I had no idea what they were doing. They wrote some words that contained sexual material and foul language which offended her. She immediately took the letter to the principal's office and showed him. Although I had no idea that they had done this, I was called into the principal's office and reprimanded for it. I was embarrassed and shocked that my friends would do this to me. I explained to the principal that I had no knowledge of what my friends had done. He understood and told me he would have the girl come in so that I could explain it to her and apologize to her, which I did.

It is sad that so many of us think so little about how we treat people. What they wrote to the girl was offensive and totally uncalled for. At that time I thought it was funny and maybe was hoping that that letter would have helped me get to know her better—not for the good, but for the wrong reasons. It's strange the way a person who doesn't know Jesus can think. I was no different than they were. I was just older and far less than wiser. I have to admit I had a strong sex drive, and because of my sex drive my understanding of love was becoming distorted. I'm not sure I can even use the word love to describe the desires I felt at that time. The lustful heart is only self-seeking, it seeks only to fulfill its own desires and satisfy its own needs. True love denies itself. I realize now that my love back then was not love, but a form of self-love. It would not be until my conversion that I would get the first glimpse of true love.

16

Hagar: A Victim of a Dysfunctional Family

While I was still a postgraduate, I met a girl named Hagar who, along with her mother, attended the same prayer group my mother used to attend. My mother left the prayer group because she felt too many people just attended so that they could be heard and perceived as messengers of God. Hagar and her mother also attended the same church my family belonged to. I had a friend who attended the prayer group regularly and on occasion he would ask me to attend the prayer meeting with him, which I always refused. One day, he suggested that there were some girls I might be interested in. At that time I was interested in meeting a girl with no concern for knowing the Lord, so I accepted his offer. I sat through the meeting and noticed Hagar and her mother, singing and praising the Lord. In my mind, I had hopes of meeting her. My soul was thirsting to be loved, not just to satisfy my sexual desires, but to be wanted by someone who would love me.

After the prayer meeting, I walked up to Hagar and introduced myself. We began talking to each other about the things of God, which I knew nothing about. I decided to ask her to go on a date, not knowing the depth of her soul that was covered up by an image of a Christian girl who was blinded to herself. I had perceived Hagar to be someone who loved the Lord, and in that understanding I was counting on her to be someone I could trust in having good morals and principles. I was also attracted to her physically because I found her looks and body desirable, hoping in the near future in our relationship that we would engage in sexual relations. To my surprise, Hagar agreed to go on a date with me, and arrangements were made for our first date.

I do not recall our first date, but I do remember our second date. We were parked in a gravel pit, sitting in the front seat of my car, talking. Hagar began to seduce me, and eventually we ended up in the backseat of the car and began engaging in sexual relations. The reason I gave in so easily to her seduction was because she told me she was unable to get pregnant due to a physical issue, which I believed, and her seduction was so powerful that I couldn't think of anything else. I had no contraceptives nor concerns about getting her pregnant, because I was unable to make a rational decision at that point. After we had sex and I began to get dressed, fear began to settle in my mind about Hagar getting pregnant, even though she had assured me she could not. I told Hagar I needed to get some fresh air and decided to get out of the car. Fear overpowered me. I began to call myself stupid, wondering how I could have been so foolish. I fell to my knees, realizing what I had just done, and I began to pray asking the Lord to keep Hagar from getting pregnant. Even though I was far from the Lord, which I did not know at that time, I still petitioned to Him, thinking in my mind He would be listening. As I was praying, I was thinking of how this would break my mother's heart. My mother always thought that all of her sons would wait until they were married before engaging in sexual relationships.

We dated for almost a year and a quarter. I was almost twenty years of age when our relationship began and Hagar led me to believe she was eighteen. I found out later in our relationship that she was not eighteen but a few years younger. I now had concerns about dating an underaged girl and getting into trouble for it, so we decided to keep it a secret as we continued our relationship. The longer I dated her, the more I saw things that troubled me, but her seduction was too powerful, and I was unable to break free from it. As I got to know her family, I realized they were living sinful lives, both in lifestyle and in their conversations. One day Hagar told me about one of their Thanksgiving dinners, a time set aside to give thanks to our God. Hagar told me about how all of her immediate family were sitting at the dinner table, talking about sexual stuff when one of her uncles decided to play show and tell, which she thought was funny. I was shocked and torn between my understanding of what I considered to be a normal family and a dysfunctional family. Unfortunately, my sexual desires were too strong and I couldn't picture my life without her, so I remained in this relationship because my sexual desires were stronger than my ability to reason.

Hagar was a troubled child, disillusioned by her understanding of what love was. She existed in a world that perceived sex as love, always exposed to relatives speaking about sexual relationships. I was ignorant to children being sexually molested until one day someone brought that to my attention. I now wonder if Hagar was sexually molested, as I try to make sense of the household that made no sense to me years ago. Hagar's mother wasted most of her days in front of a TV, thinking she knew God. Everything I saw makes me think she couldn't have known God, but possibly in her mind she felt she was close to Him. Hagar's parents spent very little time together. Most of the time her father kept to himself, a man of few words. His wife often commented about her father having a girlfriend. I always wondered if he was having an affair, too. Hagar's sister had married young, and she and her husband were always talking and thinking about sex. Hagar's brother, at times, was sensitive and at other times would have violent outbursts, which led me to believe he was possibly bipolar. He also perceived sexual relationships as the rest of the family did.

I often think of Hagar as a victim of a house in total disorder covered up by the imagery of Christ as the Master of their household. Hagar thought she knew God, but because of the instability of her mind she was as far from Him as her entire family was. To help you understand how distorted Hagar's mind was by her sexual desires, and to give you an understanding of her ability to seduce, I will share this story: I was too ashamed to walk into a drugstore to pick up contraceptives at the time. I always asked Hagar to go into the store and pick them up for me, which she did with great joy. One day as she walked out of the store and was walking towards the car, she pulled out a strip of contraceptives, and put them between her teeth, she had a smile on her face, as they hung down across her chin. I was feeling embarrassed and at the same time was stimulated as she walked seductively towards the car. Part of me was hoping that nobody saw her, or saw me sitting in the car, while the other part of me was gloating because of how sexy she was and I wanted others to see that.

I will never be able to describe the disorders of this family completely and will make no attempt to explain it. Back then I could not see, nor understand how dysfunctional Hagar's family was, because I was blinded to it by my lustful heart and my lack of understanding of God. The hardest thing for me today is to realize that there are so many families that are similar to Hagar's family—they claim to have Christ in their lives, yet live like Hagar's family.

Hagar's desire to fall in love was stronger than mine, and she yielded to her fantasies and found another man while we were still dating. She eventually broke off our relationship. After our breakup, I felt so empty and alone, and my need for sex was burning inside me. There was no one else I knew who could satisfy it. Also, at the same time, the thought of someone else having sex with Hagar was eating me up inside—it made me sick to my stomach. Eventually it all passed, as time heals all wounds. But even though the wounds were healed, Hagar left within my memory a taste of seduction that found root in my soul that would later emerge, consuming me.

How We Are Blinded to Our Parents' Love and Take Advantage of It

I often wonder how, being identical twins, my brother and I could be worlds apart in thinking. When we both lived at home, I always cut the grass and got up early to make my father's lunch and to spend time with him. I was really close to my father and enjoyed being with him even when I was full of anger. My brother Philip, on the other hand, did very little around the house—he was too busy living in the world with his friends and girlfriends. It didn't really bother me at first. It was only after my breakup with Hagar that I became jealous of my brother's lifestyle. I no longer had anyone I was physically close to, and my heart was longing to be loved. Emptiness flooded my soul, craving human affection, knowing she was gone, never to return. She was out satisfying her desires, while mine were being laid to rest. As I think back, Philip appeared to me to have it all and I had nothing, or so I thought. I now realize that I had my father's love and companionship, which Philip was missing out on, because Philip was gone and I was stuck at home. I was able to receive my father's love even though I was blinded to it and was able to sustain some kind of joy through my father's company. Later in my conversion, through God's grace, I would mimic the love that my father had shown me. My father, at the time, was all I had. He was the one who would always be there when I was in trouble and when I needed someone to talk to. I also didn't realize back then that my father was a fountain of love and mercy, and I could always return to him when I was in need of a drink. Without my knowledge, my father was an imitation of God's love. God was sustaining me through his love, as God was waiting for the day for me to return to Him and draw life through His love—the fountain of unending love and mercy. Because of my father's gentle heart, he always tried his best to comfort me. My parents were both always there for all of us, but it was my father who was the one that talked to us when we were in trouble. My mother was the firm one, and had to be; my father was the gentle one. Together they kept us balanced, as best as they could. All of my brothers feel the same way about our parents.

As children, we knew how to manipulate the system. I remember that I wanted to buy a motorcycle and my mother was against it. I was able to convince my father, behind my mother's back, to allow me to buy it. That was a selfish thing to do, but I didn't care at the time. All I knew was that I wanted a motorcycle and I would do what I had to do to achieve this. My mother was very hurt because my father allowed me to buy the motorcycle behind her back, and because, in her eyes motorcycles were dangerous. I did something very wrong because I convinced my father to betray her trust. How often children use one parent to accomplish their selfish needs without any consideration of the damage they cause their parents. I thought nothing about the strain it would put on their relationship. All that mattered at that time was to get what I wanted. Oh, my selfish soul, how empty you are—an empty barrel in need of the refreshing waters of love!

I remember my mother spoke very little to my father for weeks. In my selfish nature, all I wanted at that time was to satisfy my own needs regardless of the pain I caused others. My father loved us and I took advantage of that love. My mother also loved us, but her love contained a disciplinary nature which I now understand is necessary for an individual who wishes to move towards a more perfect love. Her ability to discipline us properly kept us balanced in the understanding that we can't have everything we want just because we want it. I feel my father's love for us was sincere of heart, but it allowed us to feed more into our selfish nature. As parents, we think by doing more for our children we are helping them out, but in reality we are feeding them the food of self-love. Because I knew that my father would do anything to make us happy, I used his love for my own personal gain and, in my selfishness, I was blinded to the pain that it would cause my mother. I took advantage of my father's love without caring.

Prior to my conversion, I did the same thing my father did—allowing my children to manipulate me. It caused division between my wife, Mary, and me. Mary constantly reminded me that I was spoiling the children and that I would pay someday for doing that. She was right. At the time, I was trying to be their friend more than a father, neglecting my duties as a father. My children always came to me when they wanted me to buy them something or take them somewhere because they knew I would always say yes. On occasion, I would ask them "What did your mother say?" They would smile and say, "What you think she would say." It wasn't until my conversion that I realized God gave me a beautiful wife. I also realized that, eventually, if all goes well, my children will get married and hopefully have children. In their new life, they will be kept busy and probably have less time to visit us, and I will understand. Hopefully, they won't move far but, if they do, we will accept and respect their decision and we will put our trust in the Lord. I realize that before we had children, it was just my wife, Mary, and me, and I also realize that when our children move on, God willing, it will be just Mary and me again. So why would I betray the very person I expect to spend the rest of my life with, the one who loved me from the beginning and hopefully to the end?

18

Unable to Pinpoint the Blame and No Desire for Success

As I reflect both on the past of my home life and my new life in Jesus, I have come to this understanding and belief in my heart that it was not my home life that made me angry. I'm not really sure if I became who I was because of that incident years ago when I was robbed as a child, or if it was the environment I was exposed to. I feel in my heart that the day I was robbed caused me great pain and suffering. I know I was unable to let go of the pain and anger I felt that day and I kept giving in to those emotions. I didn't know the road of forgiveness, nor did I understand people's frailties. All I knew was to hate, and it kept building inside me. Like anything in life, if you do not "nip it in the bud," it will grow. Fortunately, I only have a faint memory of that young lady's face who jumped me and took my money years ago. I did see her later, in my young adult years, and she looked in rough shape. For some reason, I didn't have the heart to condemn her; I was able to move on. At that time, God was not part of my life and I had very little understanding of God, and yet He was still deep within me, still part of me, calling me, waiting for me.

Looking back and understanding my parents' concerns for the future for all of my brothers and myself, I'm glad they talked my brother Stephen, Philip, and myself into taking up a trade and attending a trade school. We weren't doing much with our lives after we graduated from high school. My older brother Noah and younger brother Joseph eventually got jobs working in the local post office.

After studying and completing my course in electrical, I didn't do much towards becoming an electrician. I have no regrets about learning the trade; I just didn't pursue it. My brother Philip, who studied plumbing and completed his course, did well, became a licensed plumber, and today has several licenses. I worked for a couple of electricians but never got my license. Some people say I was just too lazy to apply myself, and maybe they're right, but part of me is happy I didn't apply myself and glad I had no desire to. For some reason I didn't desire success whether due to laziness or lack of interest. Not everyone is called to be a leader in the world and yet a lot of leaders expect people to think and act as they do. My laziness or lack of interest might have saved me. I have seen a lot of people who have become successful and lose themselves to this world. I think if I were successful, I may not have desired to search for Jesus. I am not justifying my actions, I just don't have an answer for why I didn't desire to do anything with my life. And in the eyes of a world that thinks that worldly success is everything, I may appear to be nothing, but I have found in my nothingness that true success is measured by one's capacity to love and not by the things one loves. If success is measured in the material things we possess, then our success connects back to only ourselves, and because it connects back to ourselves, it moves inward, feeding our selfish nature. I'm glad that successful people can provide jobs for many, resulting in individuals providing for their family. But with success comes pride and temptation, leaving an individual a more difficult battle for the salvation of their soul. To me, success is measured by love because love moves outward. When we do things out of love, we deny our selfish natures and someone else benefits from our act of love, therefore moving outwardly away from us. The more we love, the more it continues to move outward with the possibility of reaching the ends of the earth.

A Woman Named Mary

After I worked at a gas station operating a cash register and working for a couple of electricians, I ended up working for an aerospace company in Connecticut as a maintenance electrician. They did a lot of military work and made a lot of helicopter parts. I worked there for five years. First, I want to tell you about my wife, Mary, who I met while I was an electrician before I started working for the aerospace company. Afterwards, I will return to some of the events that happened in my life while I was at the aerospace company. I met my wife, Mary, through an ex-girlfriend of my brother. My brother's ex-girlfriend was lonely and needed a friend, and I felt the same way. I knew her fairly well because we all hung out together when my brother was dating her. So, after their breakup, I tried to console her and we ended up becoming good friends. We felt no attraction for each other—I think she wanted me to help her get back together with my brother, which I was unable to do. Regardless of the reason, we became good friends.

My friend and I would, on occasion, go out together for a drink or two—nothing special, just a social drink. One night we had decided to go out together for a couple of drinks, but she was unable to find a babysitter. At times it was difficult for her to find a babysitter because she was divorced and had three children. Somehow she found out about Mary from one of her sisters who heard that Mary babysat for other people on occasion. My friend called Mary, and she came down to watch her children while we went out. When we got back from the bar, all of us sat at the kitchen table and talked for a little while. Eventually the night came to an end, and we brought Mary home. I remember having feelings for her at that time and trying to figure out a way to ask her out. I can't remember the details of what happened next. I think a couple of weeks later, my friend had a party at her house and invited a few people, including Mary. I remember my brother Philip and a few others attended the party and we had a good time drinking and getting to know each other. Everything went smoothly without any arguments, unlike some parties when people get too drunk and start arguing and fighting with each other. The night flew by as they always do when you're falling in love with someone. Eventually the night came to an end and everyone went home. I was unable to get Mary off my mind—there was something about her. I was impressed because she dressed conservatively and, even though she was shy, I found myself being drawn to her. In the past, I had always been drawn to women who dressed less conservatively and were very outspoken.

Sometime later, my friend and I went out for drinks at a place in Massachusetts. I was telling my friend that I liked Mary and would like to go on a date with her. She was happy for me and told me to give Mary a call. After a few drinks, I finally got up the courage to call Mary that night for a date. I had had quite a bit to drink, and I was drunk. I told my friend that Mary accepted my invitation to go out, so we decided to go our separate ways; she went home and I went to Mary's house to pick her up. Back then, before I could go on a date with Mary, I had to go into the house to meet her father. When I met him, we sat at the kitchen table and conversed a little while waiting for Mary to get ready. To this day, I wonder how I got out the door without her father knowing I was drunk. We got in my car and drove to a bar in Connecticut. We walked in, sat down at a table, had a few drinks together and talked about things—just small talk. I really enjoyed Mary's company and I thought she had a beautiful smile. She was shy, but very bubbly, and easy-going. As it got late, we both realized I was too drunk to drive home, so Mary drove us to her house. When we both got out of the car, Mary asked me if I would be okay driving home. I told her I would be fine and not to worry. We said our goodbyes, I got into my car, and miraculously made it home. As I think back, I know in my heart how many times the good Lord was watching over me. I think most of us can say that God watches over all of us. Just think of how often things could have gone wrong, or how different our lives could have been if God was not there watching over us. Eventually that bar in Connecticut where Mary and I went on our first date burned to the ground. I'm not sure why it did; I think it was an electrical fire. All I know is that we will never be able to return to the place of our first date to reminisce.

Mary decided to go steady with me which made me very happy. What surprised me most about her was how shy she was. I remember when we first started dating, and the night came to an end, I would drop Mary off at her house. While parked in her driveway, I would lean over to give her a kiss, she would open up the door in a hurry, get out of the car, and wave goodbye to me through the window of my car. At first I was shocked, but as I pondered it, I felt in my heart she had great morals. I was pleased that she was shy, as I was hoping to marry someone I could trust. Mary had a cuteness about her that drew me closer to her, allowing me to fall in love with her.

The Desire to be Different and the Fire of Mary

I didn't know that Mary, in her mind, had plans to clean me up to improve my appearance. Mary had seen my brother Philip at that first party and when she saw how nicely groomed and dressed he was, she realized that she could help me. She began by helping me pick out nicer clothes and encouraged me to go to a salon for haircuts. My appearances changed drastically with Mary's help, and I have to admit she knew what she was doing.

We were not dating long when an incident in my life showed me a side of Mary that I didn't know about—I call it "the fire of Mary." Within this beautiful soul is a temper that you don't want to be around when it goes off. One day we were driving towards my parents' house and were stuck behind a school bus. I'm mechanically inclined and had built a device that mounted on the front of my car which caused lights to flash back-and-forth like a car I saw on a popular TV series. I had a button inside the car that I pressed to activate the lights and I decided to put them on behind the school bus, not knowing a police car was heading towards me from the opposite direction. As the police officer was driving by, he noticed my lights, and immediately turned around and pulled me over. He approached my window as I was rolling it down, looked inside the car at me, and asked me the purpose of these lights. I had no answer for him. He asked me for my license and registration. I pulled out my license and asked Mary to get my registration out of my glove compartment. When she opened the door of my glove compartment, a small pipe bomb rolled out onto the floor at her feet. The police officer immediately pulled his gun out of his holder and pointed it at the side of my head and told me to get out of the car slowly, which I did. He ordered me to put my hands on the car and he frisked me, then made me put my hands behind my back and handcuffed me. He put me into the back of his cruiser, and drove me to the police station, while Mary was left behind. I was shocked by how he treated me, I think because he was a rookie police officer, he overreacted, I can understand his concern, but I felt he should have realized I wasn't a terrorist: I was just a kid who liked bigger firecrackers. Back then, that's what we did. It wasn't legal, but people turn their backs and pretended not to see anything.

Mary went to my parents' house to tell my father, unknown to me, and offered to go to the police station to pick me up. When I arrived at the police station, I was fingerprinted and my photo was taken. Then I was stripped down to my underwear and thrown in a cold cell awaiting the arrival of a bomb squad to dismantle the bomb and interrogate me. It was around Christmas and the cell was cold. I was told I wasn't allowed a blanket in case I decided to hang myself. I waited for my release. Meanwhile, Mary was upstairs waiting for me, and she waited as patiently as she could for at least a couple of hours. Then the "fire of Mary" unleashed upon the officer who arrested me. She held nothing back, and her final words as she was heading out the door was to wish the officer a Merry Christmas with foul language. She got into my car and drove to my parents house to ask my father to pick me up and take me home after everything was resolved.

After Mary's departure, the officer came down to my cell, furious at what Mary had said to him. He told me he should have thrown her into the cell next to me, but my heart was cold, and his words never pierced it. I looked him in the eye, letting him know that I couldn't care less about what he had to say or thought, so he turned around and left me alone, awaiting the arrival of the bomb squad. Shortly after, another officer came down, told me to get dressed, and to go upstairs with him to meet with the bomb squad officers. While meeting with them, they realized that the entire situation was an overreaction. No bond was posted, and I was allowed to go home with my father, but had to appear in court the next day. As we were driving home, my father asked me what I was doing with the pipe bomb. I lied to him, and told him I put them into my model rockets when they were no good.

The next day, I had to appear in court before a judge, and my father decided to represent me. We sat in court, waiting anxiously for my turn. When my case was called, my father stood up and addressed the judge. The judge looked at my father and saw his brokenness—a man ashamed of being there because of me. My father, in his humility, humbled himself before the judge, pouring out his soul to the court about his son, whom he loved and believed was good. I'm in tears today thinking of the pain my father felt that day because of the shame I brought to him. The judge seeing the broken man before him and the love he had for his son, and understanding that the pipe bomb was not going to be used for acts of terrorism, was willing to dismiss my case. Unfortunately, before he could dismiss the case, the court's prosecutor stood up and argued that it was too serious a case and that I needed a lawyer to represent me. The case was extended until I could get a lawyer. I believe that the judge, out of respect for the prosecutor, agreed, knowing in his heart that this was foolishness. However, a date was set for me to return to court with a lawyer, and my father, being a good man, thanked the judge before we left the courthouse and went home.

Within hours of my being pulled over and arrested, the local newspapers had gotten wind of my arrest, and published it in the local newspapers. I was working at the aerospace company at the time and they had government contracts for the military. The next day I arrived at work and I was told to report to my supervisor's office because he wanted to talk to me. I went, sat down in a chair, and waited to hear what he had to say. He presented me with the newspaper article which I hadn't seen yet. I read it and was speechless. Giving him the newspaper back, I asked him what this would mean for me. He said, "You know I like you, Dave, but if you're convicted of a felony, I'll have to dismiss you." I told him I understood, but now I was concerned about losing my job—it was riding on the decision the court would make about this incident.

I continued working as time passed slowly, waiting for some resolution. I now had the reputation of being the "Connecticut Bomber." Mary's parents were concerned about our dating, so I had to patch things up with them. I brought shame to my family, and people in our church began to wonder what kind of child my parents had raised. The world, in its ignorance, can cause good people undeserved suffering. My parents were known as good people but it wasn't enough, as people continued blaming them for who I was. The human eye only sees the exterior of someone without understanding the true source of their trouble, but the soul that knows God can discern good from evil in an individual—not from the outside, but from the inside—because it understands its own human frailty.

The day scheduled for me to appear in court finally came. I had my father and my lawyer with me. We entered the courtroom, sat down, and waited for my case to be called. I was feeling anxious even though my lawyer assured me everything would be okay. There was so much resting on the judge's decision. My name was called and we stood up. My lawyer spoke very few words and his words sounded very similar to the words my father had spoken when we were first in court. He even spoke fewer words than my father. The judge looked at us and, without hesitation, dismissed the case as a misdemeanor, retitling it as possession of fireworks. He ordered me to meet with a probation officer to make arrangements with him for my probation. It was then that my father and I realized that it was all about the money: judges and lawyers, all watching out for each other. It wasn't about justice at all. It was about filling a friend's pocket—a sad reality.

I went to meet with the probation officer and, as we were sitting in his office discussing my case and how often we should meet, I told him that this was foolish and a waste of my time. Anyone with common sense could tell that I wasn't a terrorist and I wasn't going around blowing up buildings. The size of the pipe bomb couldn't even do very much damage. As a result, he agreed to allow me to simply come back in one year to meet with him.

A little over a year passed and, unfortunately, I forgot all about my probation meeting. I received a phone call about it, so I made arrangements to meet with the probation officer at his office to discuss the matter. When I arrived at his office, he began to tell me how much trouble I would be in because of my having missed a meeting. I told him I had forgotten about it because it was meaningless to me. We both knew it was all about my hiring a lawyer so that someone could make money. I also told him it was totally unnecessary for me to even have been put on probation. He probably realized I was right and decided to terminate my probation. I found out years later that the probation officer I had met with was arrested for soliciting sexual favors from his clients in exchange for reducing their probation time. A soul in perversion struggles in its battle to free itself from its desires, only to go back and feed itself with foods of lust, and when the food is gone, it hungers again, always hungry, never satisfied.

After high school, and as a young adult I had a desire for bombs, guns, knives, military tanks, battleships, fighting planes, and weapons of war. There was something about them that fascinated me. Was there a hidden desire for power and fear connected to my fascination for these things? Were these the stimulants that my soul desired to feed upon, necessary for the person I was and was becoming? I know that throughout my high school years and up to the day of my conversion I always wanted the respect of people and, in order to accomplish this, I created a fear in them. The image I created in high school was necessary for me to survive, so I created an image of an off-the-wall person who you did not want to mess with, and I carried the tough guy image to the day of my conversion.

Part of me was moved by Mary's fire, because within the fire was authority and power, and the same spirit dwelled within me. I think Mary was drawn to me by my tough guy image. But, deep within us, we were both sensitive and caring individuals who wanted to be loved and, contained within our souls, was the foundation of God and an understanding of commitment.

Book 2

MARRIED LIFE AND HUMAN WEAKNESSES

1

Marriage and Weak Faith

Mary and I fell in love and decided to be married. Mary was a Protestant, attending a Pentecostal church, and Mary's father was a devout Protestant. I'm not sure if he ever tried to convert me, but he would talk to me about Jesus on occasion and had a poster on his refrigerator of his do's and don'ts. Out of respect I would listen to him, but in my mind it didn't matter—Jesus was the furthest thing from my mind. I still attended the Catholic church I belonged to at the time to keep my parents happy, and because I didn't want to hear them complaining. I was just a Catholic going through the motions, fulfilling an obligation, never knowing God. I was a blind man claiming I could see, having all the answers, thinking I had it all figured out, too proud to hear anyone's input about Jesus, as a lot of Catholics are today. Each week after attending Mass at my church, I would go to Mary's church to attend her service with her. I found it to be strange, long, and boring, but I did this because I was in love with Mary and wanted to make her happy.

As our wedding day drew closer, we decided to approach Mary's pastor to see if he would marry us in Mary's church with a priest present. I didn't know the rules back then and was not quite sure if a priest would have agreed to be part of our wedding ceremony. In the end it didn't matter. The pastor refused to marry Mary and me because, when he asked us in which denomination we were going to raise our children, we honestly couldn't answer him. We weren't strong enough in our own faith—how could we decide in which faith our children would be raised? I think God answered my mother's prayers, because she wanted a Catholic wedding. We did eventually decide to get married in a Catholic church in Massachusetts. We met with the pastor of my church who agreed to marry us. Unfortunately, he was transferred to another parish part-way through our counseling, and we ended up meeting with a new priest who finished counseling and preparing us for marriage. We had to attend a few meetings to help us grow in our understanding of God, our impending marriage, and the importance of marriage. We also attended a weekend marriage seminar which was required of all couples. We completed the course and counseling and were married in the Catholic Church.

My wife always reminds me of how long the aisle was, and every so often, of how her father wanted to make sure she truly wanted to marry me. He took the commitment of marriage very seriously. I wonder if I will ask my daughter the same question when her time comes. Our wedding was on April 13, 1985 and our reception was at a banquet hall in Massachusetts. We invited almost two hundred people to our wedding and had a great time. We were very happy. Years later, the hall our reception was held in also burned down. As strange as it seems, we only have memories and some pictures of our reception hall, and we have no pictures of where we had our first date. These two places were very much a part of our lives, and it sometimes saddens my wife that we have no place to return to and reminisce. I gave up trying to figure this out. I have my own theory about how we sometimes hold onto things too much, whether in the material sense, or in our memories. All I know for sure is that two places that were a part of our lives are now gone and they will never return. I try to live in the moment, which is what I believe God wants. I am not against memories, I have just chosen not to dwell on them. I feel if I am to do the will of God, I will have to focus on the present and not the past. I will exist in the moment trying to do the best I can in that moment, knowing that everything I do becomes permanently written in the past, knowing I will never be able to enter the future because I must always remain in the moment.

We started off in a three room apartment which was in the basement of a four family home that my father owned in Massachusetts. We didn't have a honeymoon at that time because we were still moving into our apartment. We were close to my brother-in-law and his wife who helped us move into the apartment. We would get together with them often and always had a great time together. As I think back to those times in my life, I understand how sin was taking root and growing inside me. It was consuming me and the new me that Mary helped create was now elevated with pride and vanity. Those sins, along with the anger I was carrying from my past, allowed me to head down the road that was leading me to destruction and I had no understanding of it; I was blinded.

I believe a person can still live a normal life and enjoy it in the worldly sense as I did in the beginning of my marriage. But the person who lives completely in the worldly sense dies to the spiritual world and loses his ability to unite with God in a deeper intimacy. My worldly lifestyle was separating me from God and I didn't realize there was a separation. I was enjoying my wife and the things of this world and thought I was very happy. It would not be until years after my conversion that I would understand this concept.

Our First Child, a House and my Deeper Sins

I remember spending many nights with my brother-in-law, too, drinking, playing video games, and laughing late into the night. We would all party together and had a great time. This lasted for years. I'm not sure when Mary and I stopped going to church—the more we partied, the less we thought about church and the need for it. All I know is that when we did stop attending church, our souls began to drift away from God. We were blinded and had no idea that we were doing this. The devil is clever and deceives many individuals, slowly taking them away from God and, over time, they fall away from their faith. The devil creates an environment so appealing to many individuals that they slowly stop thinking about God and, before they know it, they're no longer attending church, thinking it is unnecessary. The knowledge of God fades from their memory and their soul fades away from God.

We were married a little under a year when Mary got pregnant with our daughter, Ruth. I was still working at the aerospace company in Connecticut and Mary was working at an envelope company in Massachusetts. My father, in his wisdom, talked me into building a house on property he owned in Connecticut. He told me to do it while I was still young and before I had a family. He also said it would be too difficult for me to do it later because I would be older with a family and I would have less time to build a house. At first, my wife was reluctant because she was afraid we would have to give up our lifestyle which included financial freedom and partying with our friends. I finally persuaded Mary to my point-of-view, and we began building the house. It was a lot of work for me because I was working on the house during the day and working at the aerospace company second-shift—from four in the afternoon until twelve-thirty in the morning—but it was worth it.

I saw a lot of things at the company that troubled me. Many of my co-workers' personalities conflicted with mine, making it next to impossible to find common ground to have a conversation. I also struggled with getting along with many of those in my department, Maintenance, partly because I was an arrogant and selfish individual who wanted everything my way. The sad reality is, I never saw myself at that time to be that way. I saw everyone else's faults and failures but never my own. When I looked at most of the other employees, I considered their lives to be twisted and disordered and I found their language offensive. The best way to understand this thinking is by sharing a story which I was told after my conversion. A story about two thieves. If you put two thieves in a house together and one thief steals from the other, the first thief thinks he's done nothing wrong.

34

However, if the second thief steals from him, he thinks that thief has done something seriously wrong. How often our perceptions of ourselves differ from the perceptions of those around us. We are all somewhat blinded to ourselves. We tolerated each other because I needed a job and they needed a responsible worker. I was a good worker and did everything they asked of me. The sad part was that working in maintenance made me lazy—we worked very little, and at first I struggled with that, but slowly adjusted, becoming lazier by the day. We had a lot of idle time on second shift while the rest of the plant worked continuously. Sometimes we would joke around, play cards, maybe even hide for a little while out of people's sight so we wouldn't be reported to our supervisors. There were also other things I didn't approve of at my company: there were people having affairs and sex seemed to be the topic of the day. Naked women on calendars in tool cribs and constant conversation about sex was common. I had my own problems with how I perceived sex and these things were adding fuel to my inner desires. Unfortunately, being in that environment only made my perception worse. People thought nothing of sharing pornography and were not embarrassed to talk about it, even showing it around. It was just a place of sin. As I'm thinking back, there were only two individuals that I met the entire time I was there who attended church—in a factory that employed hundreds.

In the world today, it's even worse than when I was at the aerospace company. So many men and women have lost their souls to sexual sin because of the accessibility to pornography on the internet. After I left the aerospace company and prior to my conversion, I distributed porn magazines that were given to me by friends who received ten free magazines of their choice every week. I carry the guilt of what I did because I personally know an individual who struggles with porn today because of the magazines I gave him years ago. At that time I did not know the damage that it would cause, or how addictive it can be. I pray for this individual, and many others, hoping that God will give them the grace necessary to be freed from this addiction. When I came to my conversion, I had to struggle with sexual sin, trying to erase those images deep within my memory, which would often surface without warning, exciting my senses, causing me to fantasize, and creating an urge to satisfy my sexual desires. I spent many years pleading to our Lord for the grace to help me overcome this weakness; it was a humbling experience, necessary to break my pride.

Pornography can be very addictive and creates a false image of what we think a woman should be. It also creates a false image of how we perceive sex. I felt like a prisoner to sexual sin and it was a torment to my mind and soul which, unless you've experienced it, you won't understand. But I stayed persistent in prayer and God's grace continued to strengthen me and give me hope. I believe in my heart that someday I will be free of sexual desires which is a goal I'd like to attain, not because I don't love my wife, but because I want to love her with a purer, unselfish love. My wife had surgery years ago which affected her internally, leaving her numb during sexual relations. It's made it difficult for her to enjoy such relationships and I don't want to be a burden to her; I love her enough to ask

God for the grace to achieve this. Only by God's grace can one be freed from the lies of the way the world perceives sex. God intended sex to be beautiful and not perverted; it is humans who have warped it.

Our daughter, Ruth, was born on December 15, 1986 while we were still living in our three room apartment. I continued working at the aerospace company and building the house, making it impossible for me to help Mary with Ruth. After having Ruth, our apartment appeared smaller and was always cluttered. Mary absolutely hated this and constantly reminded me about it, which put more pressure on me to finish the house faster. Eventually, we moved into our house in Connecticut in May of 1987. We were excited about our new home and fell in love with it. The neighborhood was quiet with very little traffic and the house had plenty of room to raise a family. I remember the apartment had been difficult for us to adjust to because we both came from rural neighborhoods. It was located so close to our neighbors' apartments that you could see right through their windows and it felt as if you were in the room with them. People, on occasion, were noisy when they were arguing with each other, sometimes swearing with no regard for the neighbors around them. It was the kind of neighborhood you did not want to raise a family in.

I remember as a young boy my father would take me with him from time-to-time to the complex to collect rent, and people were so kind and courteous. His tenants would shovel the sidewalks and driveway because they were happy and appreciative that they had a place to stay. At the time, the neighborhood seemed like a giant family watching out for each other, always trying to help each other out when anyone needed it. The neighborhood has changed a lot from that time and continues to change. It's been over thirty years since I've lived there. Every so often I drive by to check it out, but I'm saddened by what I see. When Mary and I were living there, we never heard about any drug problems, but today drugs run rampant in the neighborhood, and drug dealers are everywhere destroying many souls and ruining lives with no regard for others. There is so much else: innocent children, searching for happiness, unable to face realities, feeling empty inside, hoping to run away within, trying to fill a void that will never be filled. The Lord was at the door awaiting their arrival, but they never showed.

A New Career with New Hopes

Meanwhile my brother Philip was doing well at the plumbing company he was working for, which did not surprise me. He knew how to get along with people and had a great work ethic. I, on the other hand, wasn't advancing or doing anything special at the aerospace company. There was talk of the company closing someday because of the condition it was in. My parents kept telling me that I had no future by staying at a "mill," which is what they considered it. They talked me into getting a job with my brother Philip's company to learn a new trade. They felt, and continue to feel, that I didn't do much with my life, and that I never applied myself to anything worthwhile. They also felt that I wasted a lot of my talent and time on foolish things, spending money foolishly, and putting nothing away for my retirement. They are right in a lot of ways, because I have wasted a lot of my talents and spent money unwisely. I was far from God, which left me blind. All I could see was "living it up," with no concerns for tomorrow. I also didn't want to be bothered with more school or advancing in the world; I just wanted to have fun and enjoy my life. I made a lot of mistakes and bad decisions, and I'm hoping and praying that God will never abandon me—that He will provide an avenue of hope for my future.

When I decided to take the job at my brother Philip's company, I had no idea that he had taken a cut in pay. He didn't tell me at the time because he knew I never would have accepted the job. I accepted the job thinking that the company was a decent place to work because he seemed happy and successful. At that time, the minimum wage was too low for me to accept; it would have been impossible for me to support a family. Philip had a compassionate heart, was still living at home, and doing well financially. He felt bad for me because I was desperate and had a family to support, so he asked his boss to allow him to take a pay cut of almost five dollars an hour which then was added to my wages. His boss agreed to do this.

The manager of my new company was an arrogant, foul mouthed individual who treated everybody like dirt. He thought nothing of screaming at you and making you feel lowly. His thinking was that everyone is replaceable and that plumbers are a dime a dozen. Unfortunately, I believe to this day that my brother Philip picked up some of our manager's way of thinking. My brother has a kind heart outside of work, but sometimes, at work, he can be hard on you. At times, my brother reminds me of his old boss, and no matter how many times I've tried to talk to him, he doesn't want to hear it or even try to understand where I'm coming from. I make no claim to being perfect—I just believe in human dignity and respect. In the past, before my conversion, I was never able to get along with my brother at work because of my arrogance, my stupidity, and my drinking problem. I accept full responsibility for being horrible to him, his wife, and other employees who quit because of me. Since my conversion, my brother and I still struggle with getting along with each other; not because of my past drinking and bad attitude, but in a different way—because of my religious convictions and belief in human respect and dignity. I believe in my heart that my brother struggles with pride, leaving him close-minded at times. I also think he perceives me as some kind of righteous judge who goes around condemning people. I've tried to explain to my brother that my new understanding of my past failings has given me a greater understanding of other people's failings, which I know can cause them misery. I also realize none of us are perfect, but we should be open to another individual's ability to help us see our faults, otherwise we might not be able to see them ourselves. Somehow my brother Philip and I get through the day—I'm not quite sure how we do it, but we do it.

I was working for the plumbing company for approximately nine months when I fell off some staging from about eighteen feet up. It was winter and because I was numb from the cold when I hit the ground below, I felt a little discomfort, but not much. It was a miracle I survived the fall. The boss on the job saw me fall, helped me up, and asked me if I was okay. I told him I felt some discomfort and felt I should go to the hospital. He agreed. He told me not to worry about my tools and that he would pick them up for me, which he did. I was able to get into my car and drive myself to the hospital because my boss felt confident that I was okay. I allowed him to believe this because I was too proud to ask for help. As I was driving to the hospital, I turned the car heater on, and as the car began to warm up, the discomfort I felt was turning into intense pain in both my left elbow and wrist. I began to panic as the pain got worse.

I finally arrived at the hospital, went to the emergency room, and filled out the necessary paperwork. I sat in a chair for a little while, waiting for my name to be called. Once they did, I went into the room designated for emergencies, met the doctor, and told him what had happened. The doctor then sent me for x-rays to see if anything was broken. I remember in the x-ray room the technician told me she would have to put my arm and wrist into different positions to do the x-rays. She took my arm and wrist and bent them to fit on the x-ray plate. I felt she was causing me a lot of unnecessary suffering and she didn't seem to care. I finally yelled at her because of the pain she was causing me. She tried to justify her actions, but to me she appeared to have an ice-cold heart that lacked compassion. A person who couldn't care less, and really didn't want to be there. I consider myself a person who handles pain well, but the pain she caused me seemed completely unnecessary.

After I was finished with the x-rays, the technician sent me back to the waiting room to wait for a doctor. The doctor finally came out, introduced himself, and told me that I had broken my left wrist and broken off the radial neck of my left elbow. I still feel I had gotten away with minor injuries, considering that I had fallen eighteen feet. The doctor also felt it could have been worse, and he was right. He explained to me that I needed surgery and that they would perform the surgery in the morning. He also told me that I was to have nothing to drink that night because the anesthesia they were going to give me before the procedure required an empty stomach. Unfortunately, I was somewhat sedated that night and asked the nurse on duty for some cranberry juice, which she got for me to drink. The next morning came and the anesthesiologist asked me if I had anything to drink. I told her yes. She looked at me, visibly upset, and told me they would not be able to put me under. They also informed me they would have to give me local anesthesia somewhere in the neck area. I agreed to do this which would allow me to stay awake during the whole procedure—approximately two to four hours. It took the anesthesiologist several attempts to find the area required to numb my left arm and wrist. About three hours or more into the surgery, the anesthesia began to wear off and they weren't yet finished with the surgery. Because I was awake, I began to panic and told the doctor I was feeling some pain, so they quickly sewed the incision closed, but were unable to reattach the small bone of the radial neck that had broken off. As a result of the surgery, and because they were unable to reattach the radial neck to the elbow, I lost some mobility in my left elbow. During my healing process, I was in a cast which started a little above my elbow and ran down to my fingers. Eventually, I ended up with a short cast around my wrist.

A Second Child, a New Job and Injuries

As a result of my injuries, I was out of work for a few months, bored at home with not much to do. Mary was ready for another child and, as a result, became pregnant with our second child, Samuel. Before Samuel was born, and while Mary was still working at the envelope company, we had my mother and my sister-in-law take turns watching our daughter, Ruth, because we needed a babysitter. Eventually we would have them watch Ruth and Samuel together while Mary and I both went to work. This only lasted a short time.

About nine months after I broke my elbow and wrist, I developed Carpal Tunnel Syndrome. I continued working with numbness in both of my hands and continued seeing doctors to help me try to figure out what was going on. This took nine months. Meanwhile, the company manager kept hounding me to find out what was going on. I had no answers for him. He began telling me to toughen up, and wrapped boxers' tape around my wrist, because that was what he used to do when he had the same pain. Eventually, the pain got into my shoulders and I couldn't sleep. I remember getting up several nights, in the middle of the night, and building model rockets to occupy my mind. Eventually, I was referred to a plastic surgeon who immediately diagnosed the problem. He explained to me that he was going to do a carpal tunnel decompression which would take care of all the pain I was feeling, but the recovery time would be much longer than a carpal tunnel scraping. He was an amazing doctor who treated me with compassion and respect, and to this day I am grateful to him. The procedure was a total success without any complications, and the incisions in my hands are not even noticeable.

I believe I was out of work on worker's compensation when my brother Philip left his job and started his own plumbing company. His company started to grow and he asked me if I would be interested in working for him. I talked to Mary and we decided that I should take the job in hopes of improving our lives. It was difficult at first because it was hard for me to get used to having my brother for a boss while not treating him like my brother. He made his best attempt to get along with me and to make me happy, but because of the misery of my soul, it was an impossible mission. We continued working together and tried to make the best of it. Eventually, he hired a couple more people whom I tried to bully, thinking I was the boss. It got to the point that no one wanted to work with me, and they were getting upset with him because he didn't fire me. In desperation, and to keep everyone happy, he put me on Service so that I could work by myself. My soul was being consumed by some of the deadliest sins which were turning me into someone I wasn't supposed to be. I'll confess that I struggled with all of my jobs because of my bad disposition; a disposition I believe was formed by the sins I kept feeding into, day after day, year after year. My career didn't make me who I was, my sins made me who I was. It has been very difficult for me personally, as I try to recall all the events necessary to write this book. There have been times I've sat here in tears recalling some of the events of my life, going back to my memory with my buried secrets so that you might understand the destruction of sin and the power of conversion.

Mary's Struggles and Raising Children

I am not sure of when it started exactly, but Mary was complaining about how hard it was for her to raise our two children and go to work. Mary had the right to complain because I wasn't helping her with the children. I was too blind to see—all I saw was what made me happy. I've never seen a woman who loves newborns and little children like my wife Mary and she wanted to stay home with them. Mary quit her job and became a housewife and mother. I prefer children when they're older—at the communication age. I'm not one for guessing what a child wants. We raised our children the best we could. I know we would have raised them differently if I had come to know Jesus earlier in life. I would have spent more time with my children and brought them to church. I wouldn't have focused on the things of the world, but on the things of God—not as a religious fanatic, but in the true understanding of a Christian life. Unfortunately, as my children got older, I raised them to be materialistic, giving them the understanding that if you want something in life, you have to take it because no one will do anything for you. I taught them the desire to work hard for things so that they could fill their empty voids with materialistic things. Working hard is not bad; it's the thought of working only for materialistic wealth which is wrong. We can't continue thinking true happiness is found in materialism and possessing things of this world.

Through my bad example, my children also learned about self-love and instant gratification, which I believe are the very things that deny love itself. I will always pray for my family and trust that God can repair the damage I caused because of my sinful ways.

Eventually, it seemed difficult for Mary to be home with the children all of the time, so she decided to get a part-time job during the evenings. This meant I was stuck watching the children from later in the afternoon into the night. At that time, because of who I was, it was not for me. I was too busy doing things around the house, and the last thing I wanted to do was to watch children. I was not a very good father when it came to raising our children when they were infants. I didn't feel like changing diapers and feeding them, and when they were teenagers, I acted like their friend and not their father. I was able to convince my wife to have our sister-in-law watch the children at our house while Mary was at work so that I could get things done around the house. By that time, I was good at manipulating and turning things around to my favor. I worked around the house until the children were ready for bed, making sure they were fed and clothed before I would come into the house and relieve my sister-in-law of her duties. Although I was lousy at giving my children love, God provided them with the love they needed through my sister-in-law and my wife who both adored children.

Addictions and the Price We Pay for Them

My brother-in-law joined a softball league that played on Sunday mornings. He asked me if I would be interested in playing with his team and told me the league was a lot of fun. I decided to join his team and played with him on Sunday mornings. I believe today, that was the biggest mistake I ever made. We had a great time playing ball together and after the games we would drink a beer or two. Eventually softball consumed my heart and most of my time. I was no longer playing for fun and became very competitive, which turned my brother-in-law off. Eventually his team stopped playing ball, and so did he. I continued playing ball with the determination to be the best. I also believe that this was the start of my drinking problem—one beer led to two, two became three, and three became four. Eventually I would drink six to eight beers after a game and go home and pass out on the couch for two or three hours. It took several years before I became an alcoholic and had the desire to drink every night. It was a slow process that slowly consumed me—one beer at a time, from an occasional drinker, to a person who drank every night. I wasted many Sunday mornings playing ball and drinking beer and, surprisingly enough, at first Mary was good about it. Over time, it became a problem and began to consume me and most of my time. One league could no longer satisfy me, so I decided to join another league. When I joined the second league, which was a night league, it was more competitive and a lot of the guys liked to drink after the games. So after the game, some of the players stayed, and we would drink to the point of intoxication. Once in a while, my wife would come to games and watch me play, and on occasion had a beer or two with us. The field we played on was about five minutes from my house which made it convenient for me when I was drunk. There were nights I was so drunk that it truly was a miracle that I got home without any accidents or tickets.

I remember spending a lot of time practicing pitching because I wanted to be "great" in the eyes of the other players. I didn't realize it was only a dream. My desires for softball and weightlifting consumed my heart, like a fire consuming a forest. I spent every free moment that was available practicing both. My ego took control of my desires, leaving me unable to see the reality of my selfish love. And, because I wanted to be the best, I would not settle for less. I spent most of my softball career chasing that imaginary dream. I was blinded by my ego denying the truth that I was just an average softball player. I can't describe my blindness and my foolish desire to be the best; I was unable to see my limitations. I wanted the praise of everyone around me and I wanted them to look at me as a great softball player. In my mind, which was deceived by my ego, I believed that I was a great pitcher and home run hitter. It was not until after my conversion that I realized I was good, but not the best. Nothing really special, just an average ballplayer.

One day I was on the pitcher's mound practicing pitching with a friend who was catching for me, along with a couple of other people who were practicing with us. One of the guys pretended to run from first to second base. When the catcher saw him and went to throw him out at second, he accidentally slipped in a hole near home plate. Because he was throwing the softball as hard as he could, he accidentally threw the ball into the side of my ribs, injuring my spleen. I was already bent over to avoid the throw, which should have passed over my body. Immediately, I felt sick to my stomach from the impact of the softball. My friend, seeing me curled up, came running over to help me up. I lifted up my shirt to look at the side of my ribs and saw the stitch marks of the softball pressed into my skin. When I went to the emergency room at the hospital that day, the doctor on call did a few tests, then told me my spleen was swollen. I stayed a little while for a second opinion when the doctor who was to give me a second opinion came into the room. I looked up, and to my surprise, I knew him. He asked me how I was feeling and a couple of other questions, then said to me, "You're a tough guy, you can go home. There's nothing to worry about. Your spleen is slightly swollen." I asked him if I could return to work or if I had any restrictions, but he said there were none. I trusted him because I knew him and because I felt invincible. I went home, feeling a little discomfort, and thought nothing more about it.

The next day, I went to work and loaded my van for my first job of the day. When I went to pick up something heavy, out of nowhere a sharp pain pierced my stomach. Immediately I bent over in pain and was sick to my stomach. I didn't know that my spleen had ruptured. I was working for my brother Philip who saw me curled up, so he ran over to help me up, and put me in his van. He rushed me to the emergency room of the hospital down the road. They admitted me right away, did some tests, and told me I needed surgery. They asked me if I wanted the doctor they had on hand to operate, or if I had another doctor in mind. I told them I had a family doctor who also does surgery and I gave them his name. They called him immediately, then told me they had to prep me for surgery, which they did. I was brought into the surgery room, awaiting his arrival. The medical team was unaware of how badly I was bleeding internally and, by the time my doctor arrived, I had lost four to five pints of blood which had bled into the stomach area. As I was slowly fading away from this world, Hell opened its mouth in anticipation of my arrival, but God's hand wouldn't let me fall into the pit of eternal damnation. He shielded the flames of Hell from touching my body while he was appointing a servant—not a Christian, but a nonbeliever—to do His bidding. Then He breathed into the servant's ear awakening him to hurry so that he would arrive at the hospital in time to save me, a miserable sinner. Upon his arrival, God entrusted him with my life and withdrew His hand. Slowly my life was returning to my body, and my eyes opened from their slumber.

The doctor did get to the hospital just in time to stop the bleeding and remove my spleen before I died—a secret kept from me for years. I had to stay in the hospital for a few days to recover, and felt totally exhausted, not knowing why. I was also hoping I could make it to the start of the softball season. After a few days I went home, still feeling exhausted. This really troubled me and I began to think of my past surgeries, and how I felt when I was recovering from them. I remembered the other surgeries hadn't taken as long to recover. I had had surgery before, but this time it was different: I was totally exhausted and had no answers why. I found out years later about the five pints of blood that had poured into my stomach and almost cost me my life. I found out from someone I had known years before who was friendly with my brother, Philip. His wife was a nurse who had been on duty the day of my surgery. She said she remembered that day because everyone in the surgery room was panicking about the amount of blood I had lost. She also said they hadn't realized my spleen was bleeding as badly as it was. No one ever said a word to me when I was in the hospital, nor when they discharged me. She also told me they didn't want anybody to know about their "secret." It was because of the amount of blood I lost that day that it had taken my body forever to recover. I spent many days on the couch, exhausted, not knowing why, and feeling empty and useless because I had no energy to do anything. I never received a blood transfusion and I'm not sure why. It doesn't matter now—I can't change the past.

My life is different now; I don't have the energy that I used to have before I lost my spleen. Every so often, I have to get a booster shot to boost my immune system. I also have to be very careful when I catch a cold, or get sick or run down. I wish I could have my spleen back, and I also wish I had never played softball. There are many times, I wish I could've been the guy who loved to play softball for fun. Instead, I was the foolish man who played for vain and glory. Always trying to prove to the world I was somebody that I was not. It was my arrogance that drove me to do stupid things. I wasted a lot of time and neglected much of my family's needs. I didn't neglect supporting and taking care of them financially, but I wasn't the father who should have been there at his children's games: I was too busy going to games of my own. I should have been a father who spent time with his children and taken more interest in my children's and my wife's needs and interests instead of feeding my own selfish needs and desires. I can only tell them I'm sorry for not being there when I should have been. I hope and pray that I can try to make it up somehow. I can't rewrite history but, with God's grace, He can rewrite my love.

Unable to Reason Because of the Blindness of Pride

I was able to return to the softball field right when the season started. When they removed my spleen, they had to cut me through the front area of my stomach—the side where the softball hit me was all bruised and swollen, making it impossible to cut in that area. The wound was not completely healed so, in order to play softball, I had to make a strap to protect my stomach from injury and the risk of re-opening the wound. During the first game, there was a runner on first and I was on second when the batter hit the ball to the outfield, forcing me to run to third. In the hope of not being thrown out at third base, I decided to slide into third on my stomach. Unfortunately, the device I made to protect my stomach failed, and the wound opened up a little, leaving a blood stain on my shirt. The umpire took one look at my shirt, and told me to get off the field. I was upset about his decision, and argued with him about it. When I lifted up my shirt to show him the device, he told me I was crazy and ordered me off the field until the next game. I left reluctantly. I think when we're full of pride, we lack common sense. We're unable to see things for what they really are. In my arrogance, I didn't see the harm I was doing to my body, nor did I care. I felt something was being taken away from me by the umpire and felt he had no right to. However in his wisdom, he was doing what was best.

There was another occasion at a softball tournament when I was a pitcher and the ball was hit into the outfield. I went to backup the catcher as the outfielder threw the ball home, hoping to throw the runner out. The runner took out the catcher at the moment the ball arrived, and I was hit in the face by the softball, which split my lip in half. The umpire came up to me, looked at my lip, and asked me if I was okay. I told him I was fine, and proceeded back to the mound. When he asked me what I was doing, I told him I was going back to the pitchers mound. He asked me if I was stupid, and I said "No, I paid to play ball here." He told me I was insane, and ordered me off the field. I tried talking him into letting me stay, but he refused, and told me to get my lip fixed. Only then would he let me back on the field. He was probably assuming I wouldn't return, but he was wrong. I went to the emergency room, had my lip stitched up, and went back to the field, thinking he would let me play. I was wrong: he told me I was out of my mind and he wouldn't allow me back on the softball field for the rest of the weekend until after the tournament was over.

I was a proud man and did stupid things, always thinking I was some kind of superhero, always putting on a show—just crazy things that would make you question my sanity. Even my haircuts were insane—such as getting a mohawk one time. I just wanted to be the center of attention, and physical pain didn't matter. My love of softball was so powerful that it silenced my ability to reason. There were many times I would play softball with a fractured ankle and an air-cast to support it. Sometimes, after a game, I would look at my ankles and they were black and blue and swollen. I would get home and Mary would look at my ankles and tell me I was crazy. At that time Mary was beginning to question what was wrong with me, and to wonder what kind of person she had married. She was right—all the things I was doing were crazy and stupid. As I think back, I often wonder if I was insane or possessed. Regardless of my stupidity, my pride, and everything I was, my wife Mary remained faithful. Somewhere deep within her soul was the root of forgiveness and love, allowing her the ability to love even a person who was all about himself.

Moving Further Away from God and Deeper into Pride, Self-Love and Lust

While I was still playing ball, I was also lifting weights. My desire to be the best pitcher in the league consumed my heart, and I was blinded to the reality that it was unrealistic. My pride blinded me from seeing that. I was lifting weights almost every day, hoping to get stronger and better—my head was swelling with pride. I was no longer just lifting weights for softball; I began to like what my body was becoming. I would look in the mirror and be impressed with myself. My mind began to wonder—and my heart began to hope—that women would find me appealing and desirable. This led to flirting, which sometimes got me into trouble with Mary. This created an opening for me to go out partying with my friends. We'd go to bars and I'd flirt with women. Then Mary decided to go out with a couple of her friends to the bar just for drinks. We both were drifting into flirting and opening doors that were feeding into our inner need to feel loved. In a marriage this can be dangerous, because flirting can cause the mind to wander to a place it should never enter. By the grace of God, even though we were far from Him, He was still watching over us. Over time, we realized this was straining our marriage and we put an end to that foolishness. I still continued to lift weights and cut my flirting down to a minimum. I was still full of self-love and pride, unable to know the true source of love and its meaning. Mary and I loved each other in a strange way. I say "strange" only because our love for each other was a disordered love. Love outside of God is disordered in thinking. The way we had perceived love is the way the world perceives love. We both always remained faithful to each other but still loved in a disordered way. Our love was the love of the world and the things of the world. We had a great party life and a lot of partying friends. We were also sexually active, not realizing it was more lustful than it was love. We found love in materialism and bought whatever we could afford and wanted. We were in love with everything that the world had perceived as love. It would not be until years later, after my conversion, that I would begin to search for the true meaning of love, which can only be found in God, Himself.

My heart grew more restless by the day, and I missed flirting with women. One day a friend and I decided to go fishing at night and have a couple beers. I hated fishing, but decided to go anyway, just to have a couple of beers. My friend picked me up, towing his boat behind his truck, and we headed to the pond. We put the boat in the water, sat in the middle of the lake, and after a couple of beers we decided to go to a strip club. We pulled the boat out of the water, put it on the trailer, and hid it in the woods. We got into his car and drove to the strip club down the road. He had two free passes to get in, which we used. We sat at a table and were enjoying the scenery when a stripper approached our table to ask us if we wanted a private dance. I wasn't quite sure what she meant, but I was interested in it. I got up and followed her into the back room. When I looked around, I saw a bouncer who was there for her safety. She pointed to a bench where I sat down, she followed me, and stood in front of me. She removed the robe that covered her body, and began to dance in front of me, seductively. My mind began filling with impure thoughts, and I began to fantasize about her. My soul was being filled with darkness, and it was desiring intimacy with her. Thankfully within the depth of my soul was the root of faith and truth that told my mind it could not cross the line to break my marriage vows. When she finished dancing, I paid her money, left the room, grabbed my friend, and left the strip club. We went back to the lake, loaded the boat, and he dropped me off at home.

While at home, Mary asked if I had enjoyed fishing. I told her it was pretty good—I lied to her and felt no guilt. I was sitting at the kitchen table, having a couple of beers, unable to get thoughts of the stripper out of my mind. My desires needed to be fulfilled, and Mary became the vessel necessary to fulfill those desires. We entered the bedroom, with the stripper on my mind. I was taking her into the bedroom with me, not in the physical sense, but in my most inner thoughts. I was not just making love to my wife, but to the stripper, too, deep in my conscience. The flesh of one body was able to satisfy my inner hidden desire for another.

A few days had passed when I slipped up and told Mary about the night at the strip club. Mary's heart was broken, crushed by the thought that I wanted to look at another woman naked. The petals of this beautiful flower were falling off slowly, one-by-one, by the darkness that I was covering her with. She needed sunshine, which I only gave her on occasion. She continued to hope that someday I could be her shining sun. As a result of my breaking her heart, she was unable to look me in the eye for several days, and spoke very little to me. I betrayed my best friend who didn't deserve what she was going through, yet she remained strong in her love to a man who was undeserving of her love. She endured great suffering because she knew how to love. I am sorry, Mary, for what I put you through. I love you, Mary, and I always will.

Eventually I got older and joined the Jack Benny softball league which was for older men—you had to be thirty-seven or older. I continued lifting weights so that I would look really buff, hoping to impress or intimidate other players. I remember cutting the sleeves off of my softball shirts so that when I batted I could flex my muscles. I played on the same team that my brother, Noah, and my father played on. Noah could bat both left and right handed. He was also a home run hitter and was respected by all of the pitchers. I enjoyed playing softball with my family but, in my mind, I was going to surpass my brother Noah and everybody in the league as the top home run hitter.

My twin brother Philip was active at his church and its school. Once a year, the school would hold a festival and my brother would have me do the electrical wiring on his company's time. My brother and his wife were very generous to the church and the school and were well-liked and respected. On the other hand, the priests and the teachers at the school all knew me because of my arrogance—not as a church goer, because I had stopped attending church. When I was wiring for the festival, I would walk around the school and parking lot like I was a super muscle-man, thinking people will be impressed by me. This height of vanity should have been called stupidity. What had started off as something that seemed harmless, like softball and weightlifting, grew into high levels of self-love, pride, and instant gratification. It didn't matter where I was or where I went, the ugliness of my soul was craving to be noticed and wanted. I can't emphasize enough how blinded I really was to who I was. We are unable to see ourselves when we are blinded by the very things that deceive us. The deeper the deception, the worse our insight is into who we really are. Over time, we no longer know who we are, or what we have become. We're also miles away from God and what He has called us to be, as we remain blinded and continue falling away from Him. We live in a lie, and we become lost and confused, lacking knowledge of the truth, drowning in pride and self-love. I know from personal experience. I was that person.

It was because I was full of self-love that I didn't attend many of my children's activities. I went to a few of their baseball games, not because I was interested in them, but only because my wife would pester me to go and support my children, as a father should do. I understand now that I could have been a better father, but because I spent most of my time drinking and playing softball, I was unable to accomplish this. I cannot recall when my alcohol problem began; I can only tell you it slowly crept up on me, and before I knew it I had developed an addiction.

One Sunday morning, after a softball game, some of us were drinking at the softball field, getting drunk, and we eventually ended up at a bar down the road. I was so busy drinking with my friends that I forgot Mary had somewhere important she had to be. She finally got in touch with me at the bar, came in, and started lecturing me. She was furious, and rightfully so. She had no one to leave our children with and was forced to drop them off with me. She told me to go straight home and act like a responsible father. I refused to listen to her, and stayed at the bar with my children. Old foolish pride, how blind you left me; drowning in a pool of my stupidity, with no concern for my children's well-being. You are the master of ignorance and foolishness and bring shame to those who embrace you.

It was late afternoon, and I finally decided to go home. I had driven to the field with a friend in the morning and had told him I would get a ride home, not realizing I wouldn't have a ride. It was a drizzly, rainy day outside, and we had a long walk ahead of us—it was between two and three miles to our house. I left the bar with my two children and we walked home in the drizzling rain. I remember that my friend's wife drove up and asked me if I needed a ride home. I was too proud and didn't want her to know I was drunk, so I told her that I wanted to walk with the kids. She asked me if I was sure, I told her yes, she said goodbye, and drove off. When we arrived at home, we were soaking wet from the rain. As a result of my stupidity, my daughter Ruth caught a cold and was sick for a few days. Innocent children, victims of a father's selfish heart, suffered unnecessarily because of a blind man's actions.

I was a poor excuse for a father and a husband, and deserved to be abandoned by my family. God, in His mercy, forgives and allows others to forgive, even when we're not worthy of forgiveness. As I sit here with my eyes filled with tears of regret for who I was, part of me wishes I could do it all over again and rewrite the past. But, unfortunately, I can't! I know it's because of God's mercy and love that my children turned out okay, thanks be to God. The main reason only part of me wishes I could change the past is that the other part of me still needs it in order to show you the power of my conversion.

Price Paid for Sinfulness and God Calling Me Back to Him

The last few years of my softball "career" went as follows: My left knee required a total knee reconstruction, which required me to be out of work for three months. The surgery was a great success, but right before I was able to return to work, I had a heart attack which put me out of work for another three months. I eventually got back onto the softball field and played a couple more years without injury. Then one day, while I was playing shortstop, I went to catch a ball that was going into the outfield. I wanted to be a hero and dove for the ball—right into the outfielder's shin, fracturing my cheek bone. Shortly after that, while playing shortstop, a softball took a bad hop and hit me on the other cheekbone fracturing it. I saw a specialist who told me that one more hit to my face could affect my vision. I decided to wear a face mask to protect my face whenever I played ball. During my last year of softball, I accomplished my goal of leading the league in home runs and, simultaneously, reached the peak of my sinfulness. To this day, I wonder why God allowed me to accomplish this. Was it to give me the understanding that the joy I had on that day would be nothing in comparison to the joy that was to come? I'm not sure—I can only guess, in the hope of someday knowing the answer.

At this point in my life, my children were older and I was struggling with alcoholism. I think my son, Samuel, was almost out of high school and my daughter, Ruth, was attending college. I finally reached rock bottom and Mary had threatened me with divorce several times. I wanted so badly to quit drinking and tried several times, but the addiction was too strong; I just wasn't able to do it. Sometimes when I drank I would get so mean you didn't want to be in the same room with me. I was alright when I drank beer, but when I drank whiskey, I was just plain mean. I remember one night when my wife was complaining about my drinking and wouldn't let it go. Eventually, she left the room and went into the bedroom to watch TV, leaving me alone in the kitchen with a bottle of whiskey. I was furious with her because she left me alone in the kitchen. The longer I sat alone, the angrier I was getting, as the devil continued filling my head with his lies. I went into the bedroom shortly after, to argue with her some more, but she tried to ignore me and told me to leave the room. I pulled out my pistol BB gun from the top drawer of my bureau and began waving it around in front her like I was some kind of tough guy. I continued shooting off my mouth, then left the room, went back to the kitchen table, and had a couple more drinks. Guilt flooded my soul and I began to hate myself for the person I had become. I felt like a prisoner with no way out. I just wanted to free myself from alcohol, but felt so helpless—the addiction was stronger than my will. I was running out of time and options, and my wife was bearing more than she could handle.

I had a friend who I would see on a job site occasionally. He was a reborn Christian attending a church in Connecticut. He knew I was struggling with alcohol, and every so often he would talk to me about Jesus Christ. He was a nice guy, and I tried to listen to him because I was desperate and in need of help, but his words were unable to pierce my soul. I heard what he was saying, but the state of my soul wouldn't allow his words to enter. It took a lot of time and a lot of desperation before I could begin to understand what he was trying to teach me.

He kept asking me to attend one of the services at his church, but I kept putting it off, feeling in my heart I had better things to do and it would be a waste of my time. Around the same time, I had a friend down the road who didn't drink alcohol. On occasion, I would go to his house with a cooler which contained six beers and I'd drink them as I was conversing with him. One day, he was sitting in his chair, watching TV, and I walked into his house. I think it was after I had cleared his driveway of snow, which I did for him because he was unable to. I sat down on his couch and conversed with him while I was drinking the beers at a fast pace. No sooner did I finish the last beer, when he looked me in the eye and said to me "you have a drinking problem." I was shocked and didn't say a word out of respect for him because he was older. I told him I had to go, and I left his house. I walked out the door and headed home, furious, I said to myself, "Who is he to say such a thing to me, especially when I helped him out so many times in the past?" I went home, hating him, and also ashamed of myself. For the first time in my life, the wall of truth was right in front of my eyes. My pride could no longer mask the truth: I was face-to-face with it and I needed to address it. God used that moment to open my eyes to who I really was.

At this point in time, I was fully aware of my drinking problem, but was too ashamed to go to an Alcoholics Anonymous meeting. I considered going to my friend's Christian church, in the hope that God might be able to help me. I was desperate, powerless, and unable to quit drinking on my own. In my mind, I knew it was either Alcoholics Anonymous, or a miracle. I could no longer save myself. I believe God wanted me to know that so that I would know it was He, alone, who had saved me. I decided to attend the nine a.m. service at my friend's church. I got my car, drove to his church, walked in, and was greeted at the door by a parishioner. I shared with him my drinking problem. He said to me, "It will take time." As soon as he said those words, something deep within my interior spoke to me, and I could not accept his words. In this interior communication, the words he said to me appeared to be lacking something. I knew he was trying to comfort me with his words, and yet they lacked some kind of truth—as if God were speaking to my interior, letting me know that He could deliver me from alcohol, here and now, if He chose to. At that moment, I felt comforted, but I still lacked understanding. The thought of being delivered from alcohol flooded my soul, and I began to wonder if God was speaking to me interiorly. I was unable to focus on the preacher speaking at the service because these thoughts wouldn't leave my head. I couldn't stop them, no matter how hard I tried. Deep in the interior of my soul, God planted a seed that was growing, and would soon become the promise He would give me later down the road. I remained at that Christian church for four months, still struggling with alcohol. I faithfully attended the church services once a week, hoping for a miracle, and when fellow parishioners asked me how I was doing, I lied to them, telling them I was doing better, because I was too ashamed to tell them the truth.

One day, my friend showed up in my yard when I was splitting wood and asked me how I was doing. I had beer on my breath and my friend knew it. I told him I had stopped drinking. He knew I was lying and didn't say a word to me because he didn't want to discourage me or hurt my feelings. Later down the road, after my conversion, he told me that he remembered that day, and that he had smelled beer on my breath but didn't have the heart to tell me. On occasion, he reminds me of that day, and that he knew I was drinking. I'm no longer ashamed to tell people about the disease that consumed my soul, because I'm free from that torment, knowing in my heart there are many still imprisoned by it—victims that walk through a door that closed behind them, unable to get back to where they entered, as they struggle to find another way out.

Book 3

Saved from Eternal Punishment and Religious Concepts

1

God Chooses Us and an Understanding of the Interior Communication

Before I go into more details of my conversion, I want you to understand that there's a fine line drawn between humility and pride when you share your thoughts and words with other people. I've tried to humble myself as much as possible to share my past with you. As I share my conversion with you, I hope to demonstrate a fair amount of miracles which I am excited to relate to you—not so that I can boast in them, but because there was nothing I have done that was deserving of them. God, in His generosity, has granted a miserable sinner, who was undeserving of His love, miraculous gifts. I have become a child totally dependent on God. If I appear to be boasting, I'm sorry, it is not my intention. My only goal is that you see the power of God and know it is available to anyone who desires to know Him. I would like to leave you with a passage from the Bible that might help you understand that it's not we who decide the gifts that God will distribute, but He. "I give praise to you, Father, Lord of heaven and earth, for although you have hidden these things from the wise and the learned you have revealed them to the childlike." (Matthew 11:25)

I would like you to try to understand the interior communication inside the soul as I have come to understand it. It's not a thought of the mind, but something stronger. It's hard to describe, but I'll try. It's a voice with no sound—that communication to the soul. It isn't a voice that you hear, and yet it speaks with authority so that you feel confident in what it's telling you. It's God's way of speaking to you through the interior of your soul. You can't create this thought, because it's beyond a thought. When you receive this interior communication, you feel confident in acting upon it. You don't question it; you just respond to it. And when you respond to it, you'll bear the fruit of that to which you respond. For example, God might tell your interior to speak to an individual that you may not know. You won't know why you have to speak to this individual, and you'll feel uncomfortable about it. Because of human nature, you will find it difficult to respond to this interior communication for fear of rejection. But in the supernatural nature, you approach the individual out of obedience to the interior communication. And if the interior communication is a true communication from God through the Holy Spirit, then someone will benefit as a result of the action. The Holy Spirit will always give you the words necessary to speak to the individual—you won't have to rely on your own words. God uses us, allowing the Holy Spirit to speak through us, in order to strengthen individuals who might be suffering emotionally or spiritually. God may also choose to reveal something about the individual who might be suffering from a physical ailment. Whatever the revelation might be, I believe that the ultimate goal is to help this person search for God in a deeper way. Both the person receiving the interior communication and the recipient of the interior communication should benefit from these communications.

A Daughter's Cry and a Desperate Father

I was still attending the Protestant church with my friend, while my daughter was attending a different Protestant church called Christian Church in Connecticut. On several occasions, Ruth would ask me to go with her, but I kept refusing because I didn't feel like going there. The reason was that a few of the parishioners from my church knew her pastor and had nothing good to say about him. This was my first excuse for not attending a service at her church. The second was that I didn't know anyone there except for my daughter. However, I believe to this day that God allowed my daughter to find Christian Church and to attend their services while He was preparing me for my conversion.

I remember one particular day that Ruth had asked me to attend her church. As she was speaking, my soul received my second interior communication, which was, "If you go there, I will deliver you from alcohol that day." I have to admit that after receiving the first communication, I was more attentive to the second. However, I was still uncertain about it. It spoke to me from within. It was similar to the first communication I had received, but it was stronger and more convincing. It was beyond my consciousness and I became a little concerned about it. I began to wonder if I was going crazy. The voice spoke to me with tenderness and authority at the same time. The voice was calling me and I wanted to believe in it, but I was struggling with disbelief. So for the next two weeks, I battled with that interior communication, going back-and-forth wondering if it was real or not, or if I was out of my mind. I kept asking myself if God would really deliver me from alcohol—would it be that easy. I had my doubts, because I had struggled for so long and I felt it was impossible for this to be real. And yet that interior communication was too strong to ignore. It meant I would have to leave the church that I enjoyed attending and go to another church to start over again. My heart was troubled because I didn't want to leave, and my will had no intention of leaving, but God had other plans for me.

Two weeks later, I was drunk on a Saturday night, I remember the date: February 17, 2007. I was in my bed, trying to sleep, when Ruth walked into my room to see if I was awake. I was, but in somewhat of a drunken state. She looked at me, then asked if I would consider going to church with her in the morning. I looked into her eyes and saw a broken and desperate child, hoping to help her father be free of this disease. I saw the pain in her eyes and I felt her heartache. In that moment, I realized the pain I was causing my family. I could no longer accept who I was and I was ashamed. My guilt flooded my heart to the extent that selfishness and self love could not exist. Also, in that same moment, I felt God was calling me, and that He would keep His promise to me. So I agreed to go with Ruth in the morning. Ruth saw me drowning in the world of drunkenness, and in her heart she could not let me drown. I remember the joy in her eyes when I agreed to go. I'm not sure if her faith was strong enough. I think in her heart she felt that her pastor could help me with my alcohol problem. Ruth was always praising her pastor, and felt in her heart if anyone would be able to help me, it would be he. Whatever her motives were, God would use them for my conversion.

The next day, I got into my car by myself and drove to Christian Church. After our conversation, Ruth had gone to a friend's house and decided to stay overnight. As I drove, I was a little nervous and at the same time I felt some confidence in God's promise—the promise that He would deliver me from alcohol on that day. As I was pulling into the driveway, I felt a little apprehensive because it was a dance studio that was used on Sundays to hold church services. I had my doubts because I felt in my heart it really wasn't a church—I was so accustomed to attending big, beautiful churches that made me feel like I was actually in a church. How would I ever be able to explain to anyone that I worshiped in a dance studio that turned into a church on Sundays? I, myself, struggled to accept that this place was a place of worship. I realize today that God was showing me He could perform His greatest miracles in some of the simplest places. I had always associated miracles with great places because of my ignorance. I realize today that Jesus dwelt among the simple and, in the simplicity of my life, I could find Jesus in the depth of His love. I still love the beauty of the big churches—all of the artwork and paintings that has inspired so many—but I also know that God's miracles can happen anywhere, and that true faith and trust in the Lord is the greatest possession one could ask for. All you have to do is to let go of yourself and trust in God's providence. It was my faith in God's word that brought me to the doors of Christian Church.

So I walked through the doors of Christian Church and the pastor's wife greeted me. We introduced ourselves and spoke a little, then I said to her, "You're not going to believe this, but God said to me, 'If you go there, I will deliver you from alcohol that day.'" She looked at me in a strange way, and I think she was uncertain if I was crazy. I tried to explain to her what that meant, but I think she was feeling perplexed. It's not every day that someone walks through the doors of your Church with a message from God. I wonder how I would have responded if someone had said that to me.

She told me to wait there while she went off to get her husband, the pastor, probably thinking I was strange, but who knows? Maybe she believed and understood me; I can't be quite sure. She returned with her husband, who introduced himself to me. I have to admit he had a charisma about him which made me feel very comfortable. I told him the same thing I told his wife, and he seemed to accept it. We talked a little while, then he asked me if I would mind if he prayed over me. I told him of course not, and he prayed over me. I have to admit, I felt no different. He showed me around the place and introduced me to a few of his parishioners, then we went into another room where the services were held. We sat down and waited for the service to start. The service seemed like your typical Christian service. It had a music ministry and the pastor then spoke to the congregation. It was nothing out of the ordinary. I felt a joy when I left the church; not the joy of the spirit, but a joy in the human emotion which you feel when sharing with good people.

I got into my car and went home, thinking nothing of it. I didn't feel any different; it seemed to be just like any other service I had attended. I was not slain in the Spirit, nor felt the presence of Christ inside myself; I felt just like me. I think most of us expect to feel some kind of drastic change. I know I did. Without my knowing, God secretly whispered inside my soul and delivered me without my flesh being aware. God pierced my soul, and in that brief moment removed the demons that were separating me from Him. His light pierced my soul right through the darkness of myself and I never felt it. His Spirit was now within me, thriving and full of life, breathing life back into my dead soul. I invited Jesus into my heart and He entered. I hope and pray He will dwell in me forever. Amen.

The Old Man Dies and a New Man is Raised

I call this the first awakening because my soul was asleep. I was physically awake, but my soul was asleep without the knowledge of God to awaken it. Everything I was, worked against my knowing God: I was an alcoholic and a softball and weightlifting fanatic. I was full of pride and self-love. I had a foul mouth. My soul was full of sin, like a glass full of water, and something needed to be emptied to make room for the things of God. I also mumbled, but that didn't keep me from knowing God. I had mumbled since I was a child and my mother would always tell me to enunciate my words. I was just too lazy. The only time you ever heard me was when I was drinking and shooting off my mouth, which I know offended God and pushed me further from Him.

I was home for a few hours before I went downstairs to my basement to practice swinging the bat and lifting weights. I would practice these routines several times a week. I went to pick up the bat to practice my swing and I realized the desire to swing the bat was gone. At that time I thought nothing of it because sometimes I wouldn't be in the mood. So I looked at the weights and the desire to lift weights was gone, too. Next, I found myself touching my mouth, and found my mouth was silenced from using foul language. I was perplexed, and yet part of me was wondering if I had received the miracle God had promised me. At the same moment in time, I was filled with both joy and concerns. Part of me wanted so badly to believe, the other part of me was somewhat doubtful because I had never been able to quit alcohol on my own. I didn't really know God, and I felt unworthy of such a miracle.

After this experience I went upstairs, a little apprehensive about telling my wife about what had just happened. I felt it was too soon to be sure because of my doubts. I always drank before supper so that I could drink as many beers as possible before I ate. I didn't want the food to fill me up, leaving no room for alcohol. Instead, that night I had supper with Mary. I don't remember Mary's reaction to my not drinking before supper because in the past I had made it a day or two without drinking while attempting to quit, but I had always failed. All that I remember was that it was nice to be sober, and I was hoping that God would deliver me forever from the torment which had wasted so many years of my life. I cannot describe how badly I wanted to be free of alcohol. I was hopeful and concerned, and I was trying very hard to trust in God and His promise.

After supper, I excused myself and left the table, heading to my bedroom. While walking to the bedroom, I had this incredible desire to read the Bible. It was an intense feeling filled with joy, and it was strange to me because I never had the desire to read prior to my conversion. I could not believe that I had a desire to do this. All my life, I felt the Bible contained great stories, but never had an interest in reading it. I also thought of it as a complicated book that was too hard to understand, and maybe even boring. I responded to the desire to read it, anyway, and I found a Protestant Bible somewhere in the house. It had belonged to my wife from years before. I picked up the Bible, went into my bedroom, closed the door, and began to read it, unable to put it down. I found myself going into my bedroom every night after that, reading the Bible for hours at a time. At that time, I didn't know there were different versions of the Bible. I had thought everybody had the same Bible. It didn't matter—I read what I had. I would lay on my bed for hours, reading the Bible as time appeared to be passing me by swiftly. I just couldn't put it down. And as I was reading the Bible, I was amazed, because it was making complete sense to me.

I remember my wife, Mary, peeking her head through the doorway of our bedroom door from time-to-time to make sure I was okay. This lasted awhile because it was something new that Mary had never seen. I continued reading for several months, because my heart and soul desired to know God. I felt like an empty vessel that needed to be filled, but not with the things of the world, instead with the things of God. The more I read, the more God filled me with an understanding of His word and His truth. Because of my persistency and desire, I completed the Protestant Bible in eight months.

The Possibilities with God are Endless

It's a miracle in itself that a person who had never read a book in his life now had an incredible desire to read every night for months. I realize now that I needed to know God in a more personal way, and I also wanted to try to understand God as best as humanly possible through His words in the Bible. Believe me, there are a lot of things in the Bible that could be misunderstood or misused for personal gain. Personal interpretation can be dangerous and misleading and I encourage everyone to read the Bible in the simplicity of its understanding. We should never use certain lines in Scripture alone to prove our point. We should use the Scriptures in their entirety to understand God and we must rely on the help of the Church to guide us. I have come to my own understanding of God through reading the Old Testament. I have also come to my own understanding of His son, Jesus, in the New Testament, not in contradiction to the Church's teachings, but in union with the Church's teachings; just a simpler understanding. In my understanding, I feel they are both separate and yet one. I will always perceive God as a God of justice, as well as love. I perceive Jesus as the outpouring of God's love upon this earth through His crucifixion and precious blood which was shed for all so that we might have salvation. Together, along with the Holy Spirit, they form the Trinity: each unique in their own way, and yet completely one with each other.

After a couple of days had passed, I was a little nervous. I wasn't sure if what I was feeling would last, or if it did last, for how long. It was something new of which I knew nothing. I had been away from church for almost twenty years and, when I had been in church, I had never paid attention. If there was any kind of foundation, it wasn't a very strong one. Even though my background in faith was weak, I still felt some kind of reassurance inside myself. It's hard to describe—it was like a cloud of darkness was lifted from me. I felt really happy and free. I was no longer a prisoner to alcohol. The desire for alcohol appeared to have disappeared, and yet I still remained a little apprehensive. In the past, I had tried so many times to quit drinking and always failed. My memory was my biggest enemy and created doubt inside my mind—it's our human nature. In our human nature, we all have failed in something that we have tried to give up on our own.

My old self died. Who I was and everything about me died in my conversion. I no longer had the desire to drink alcohol, to play softball, to lift weights, or to use foul language. I had this intense love for God and Holy Scriptures. Within me was this new kind of love that I knew nothing about. Everything I loved in the past I no longer loved, except for my family. I was a new man in Jesus and this was quite an adjustment for Mary. I was no longer the man that she had married. The tough guy was now a gentle sheep. The man who had wasted his money foolishly became wise and appreciated his blessings from God. The man who used to sit in the living room with her and watch violent and provocative TV could no longer look at the TV. And my partying days were over. Mary was now beginning to think that life would be boring. She was looking at me as if I were some kind of Jesus fanatic. At that time, certain Christians called me a "reborn Christian," a title that I struggle with today because I feel it's definition is still unclear.

Saved But not Salvation

During my eight months at Christian Church, there would be occasional moments when a fellow Christian would approach me and ask, "Are you saved?" I was never able to answer that question completely the way they were expecting me to, because inside myself I didn't completely understand its meaning and struggled with other Christian's perception of that word. Even today, Christians continue to misinterpret being saved.

I believe that God wanted me to ponder the word "saved" later in the depth of my conversion. At this point, I realized "saved" and "salvation" were not the same word. Certain types of Christians use "saved" as one word tying "salvation" to it. I believe they're two different words with two different meanings. They seem to lack a complete understanding that when you're saved, you do not secure salvation. In my understanding, when you are saved you will come to the knowledge of Jesus Christ as Lord and Savior, but you do not secure Heaven just because you are "saved." In my understanding, "salvation" can only be determined when an individual is standing before God, Himself. God has the final word, not us. Our assuming that we have secured salvation would be like taking the words out of God's mouth. Let me try to explain. When we're standing before God to be judged, we are waiting to be judged. Now there are those religions that believe Jesus is the mediator between God and man and that Jesus is the mediator for us here on this earth and only on this earth. But I tell you, he is also our mediator when we are standing before God. And, if what I am saying is correct, when we are standing before God, Jesus will be by our side as our mediator. Picture in your mind: God is now facing you and knows your heart and what you have done, or did not do. God will then speak to you and tell you whether salvation is yours, or not. Remember Saint Paul said in the Scriptures that he had to work out his salvation with fear and trembling. He worked out his salvation, never securing it. The choice is yours: you can presume that when you are "saved" Heaven is yours, or you can see "salvation" as something that you'll work for until the day you die.

Our presumption that we are going to Heaven is a big mistake. I know when the day comes and God is calling me home, when I'm standing before Him, I'll be a little concerned. I know I constantly sin and offend God on a daily basis. I think the problem today is that we rely too much on Jesus's mercy, and think nothing of God's justice. In my opinion, to know God is to know both God's justice and His mercy. We should also try to understand the love of God through Jesus Christ, His son. For example, if a Christian lives a life totally reliant on Jesus's mercy, will this Christian tend to look at his or her sins with less fear and concern for them? And, as a result, will they live a more sinful life, abusing Jesus's mercy? On the other hand if a Christian lives in the fear of God alone, will he be able to embrace the love of Jesus Christ? Probably not. This person might never feel forgiven, or loved by God. Such an individual could never find true peace, living in the fear of God.

I encourage everyone to try to know both God's justice and Jesus's mercy in the hope of living a balanced Christian life. We should always have a respectful fear of offending God because our sins offend him. And, we should always ask for forgiveness, in the hope of embracing the love and mercy of our Lord and Savior, Jesus Christ, who is always ready to forgive us and give us the necessary graces to overcome sin. In my continuing journey, I will always have a respectful fear of offending God, and I will always embrace the love and mercy of Jesus, our Lord and Savior.

Mary and I Struggle with the New Me

The first few months of my conversion were difficult for Mary because the man she had married was dead to her, and we drifted worlds apart from each other with very little in common. Even though the things she didn't like about me were gone, the things that she did like about me seemed to have disappeared, as well. I was stripped naked before the Lord, and the things that Mary loved about me appeared to no longer exist—I was a new man in Jesus Christ and very immature to the understanding of a true Christian life. At first Mary was angry with God and wanted nothing to do with church. She thought Christians were too extreme because of her past experiences with "overboard Christians." For Mary, now her husband was one of these religious fanatics. It was also difficult for me because Mary kept talking about divorcing me. She said she refused to be married to a "Jesus freak." It wasn't making any sense to me at the time that God would change my heart, only to have my wife want to divorce me. And, to make the situation worse, God kept speaking to my interior and saying to me, "Who do you love more?" In the silence of my soul, I would always respond, "You, Lord, but this does not make sense." Then, in response, our Lord would say to my interior, "Trust me."

It was so hard for me to trust in the Lord because my marriage was struggling, and I was worried that Mary was going to divorce me. I was also feeling the weight of rejection from my family members and friends; particularly my drinking friends. They were slowly disappearing, one-by-one, because I had stopped drinking. I soon began to realize the common ground that tied my friends to me was alcohol. When my desire for alcohol disappeared, so did my friends. I felt betrayed by the shallowness of their love for me. I felt so alone, separated from the world I once loved. I was stripped of the things that possessed my heart. I no longer felt the desire to play softball, or weightlift, or drink. I was alone, but not alone. God broke the chains, and I was free, never to return to alcohol, weightlifting, or the softball field again.

Somehow Mary and I, with the grace of God, survived our trial. It's hard to describe the emptiness and separation Mary felt because of my conversion; she wasn't the one who changed, I was. The man she fell in love with no longer existed. The emptiness and shock she felt because of my conversion was so much for her to bear. It was as if her best friend had died. However in the depth of her heart, she still loved me enough to find a way to make it work. God filled Mary's soul with the necessary graces to keep us together.

Unrighteous Judgment

While I was at Christian Church, the pastor's thinking became part of my thinking. I had accepted the idea that if you don't accept Jesus Christ as your Lord and Savior you would go to Hell—there were no exceptions. Jews, Catholics who didn't have a personal relationship with Jesus—they felt Catholics didn't know Jesus and went to church only under an obligation—and anyone else who didn't accept Christ as Lord and Savior would perish. As a result of that kind of thinking, I soon became judgmental and self-righteous. Before I knew it, I was turning people away that didn't belong to Christian Church. Instead of converting them, I was condemning them. It got to the point where Mary was afraid of taking me anywhere because she was worried about what I might say to people. She would always warn me to not talk about religion with anyone. When I spoke, I spoke in judgment and condemnation and as a result, I was turning people off. They wanted nothing to do with me, or the Lord. It got to the point that wherever I would go, people would intentionally avoid me. I believe that the members of Christian Church didn't truly understand the message the Scriptures should have taught them. We were all blinded by spiritual pride and were limited in our ability to interpret them. We also lacked the true interior life necessary to achieve a deeper union with God which would help us develop a better understanding of Him and His ways.

I remember, standing in the hallway at Christian Church. One of the members was telling one of the leaders of the church about how proud he was that he was drinking a nonalcoholic beer. He was an alcoholic, trying his best to quit on his own using his own strength. The leader looked at him in a condemning way and said something like, "You need to put your trust in Jesus, and quit cold turkey." I held myself back from saying anything because I was fairly new to the church, but deep inside I felt angry and disappointed with him for being so insensitive. That poor individual was in need of support and, being a former alcoholic, I understood his struggle. I was shocked by what the leader had said to him and it bothered me the rest of the day. I asked myself how this leader could be so cold, without understanding or sympathy for this man. My soul was troubled because I couldn't see the heart of Jesus in this leader.

It would be years before I realized that many people lack compassion for those souls that fall into addictions. Before my conversion, I was one of those souls. The leader had no understanding of how innocent people, without themselves knowing, walk through the doors of darkness. How people, just out of curiosity, weakness, or even depression, will try something to fill a void in their life. And, at the same time, think they're strong enough to overcome the desire of what could easily become an addiction. Once they get a taste of it, they often have to return to it to be satisfied. Then they fall prey to their desire. Once addicted, even their innermost desire to be free cannot free them. Tragically, they're pulled in, like lambs led to the slaughter. If you've never had an addiction, you should thank God. If you have, you know the pain and the feeling of being imprisoned by your addiction. For someone with an addiction, there isn't a day that goes by that feels free. Let's try to understand and show compassion, mercy, and love for those lost souls. Jesus came for the sinners, not the righteous.

The Bible and Misinterpretation of It

I was reading the Bible every night because I had this intense desire for the Scriptures and was trying to understand God as best as the human mind could. No one on this earth can ever truly understand God and His ways. The Bible starts with the Old Testament which consists of many books written before the birth of Christ. The New Testament contains many books as well, written after the crucifixion of Christ, which contain the writings of some of the apostles and Saint Paul, and ends with the book of Revelation. Naturally, a person when reading a book, will start from the beginning and work their way to the end, which I did. I started in the beginning of the Bible and tried to work my way towards the end. Then one day, the pastor asked me to skip the Old Testament and go right into the New Testament. He wanted me to know Jesus Christ on a personal level. I believe he felt in his heart I needed to know Jesus better in order to be a better Christian. Because he was the pastor, I took his advice and began to read the New Testament. Something didn't feel right, but out of fairness to him I tried a couple of times to skip the Old Testament and read the New. I was unsuccessful because, as I was reading the New Testament, I felt myself being pulled back to the Old Testament. I tell people today that I feel God kept pulling me back to the Old Testament so that I could come to a better understanding of who God was first, before He would let me know His Son.

As true Christians, we believe in the Trinity. We don't have a total understanding of it because of its complexity. In my understanding, I see God as a just God, and know my sins offend Him. I also believe that I will answer for my sins if I choose not to repent of them and make reparation for them. I have also come to understand Jesus as the mercy and love of God, which is not to be abused and taken advantage of. I feel that many people today think nothing of sinning and offending God, because they are constantly relying on the mercy of Jesus. As a result of this thinking, I feel many people are taking advantage of and abusing Jesus's mercy.

I eventually got to the New Testament and my understanding of who Jesus Christ was and is today, which resulted in a conflict with the pastor's thinking. The pastor felt that God wanted us to have material things. I'm not talking about necessities, but the things of vanity. In my heart, I was struggling with that thinking, because I was very materialistic before my conversion. One day, the pastor and his wife came to my house for a cookout. My wife decided to tell them that I didn't want to buy her a swimming pool because of my warped understanding of God. The pastor looked me in the eye, chuckled, then told me

I was being selfish, and that I was wrong. Right in front of my wife. He also told me that God wants us to have everything and to enjoy this world to the fullest. Unfortunately, at that time, I had no knowledge of the lives of the great Saints of the Catholic Church who had sacrificed so much to live simple lives. Therefore, I was unable to support my thinking, and to debate this topic. I just felt in my heart that God didn't want me to be materialistic.

As a result of this conversation, Mary and I ended up purchasing a swimming pool, and of course she was very happy about that. I felt betrayed but I thought maybe God used that moment to break the tension between Mary and me. It was a place in the middle for the two of us to meet, and the decision didn't affect me spiritually because I wasn't the one who wanted the pool. My desire was to do God's will, and even though I was still far from knowing God interiorly, he was deep within me, guiding my heart, mind, and soul. I was spiritually blinded because I was full of self, not knowing how to die to myself, leaving me unable to know what was best for my family. I'm not against materialistic things, only against the possession they can have on your soul if abused. My first, and most important concern, for my wife and family is the salvation of their souls; everything else is secondary to that.

The Protestant Church and Spiritual Pride

I remember Mary attended a couple of services at Christian Church during the eight months that I was there, only out of her love for me, trying to make me happy. Mary struggled with Protestant churches because her father belonged to a church once that had taken advantage of him, and eventually he fell away from church altogether. Mary's mother, who makes the claim to know Jesus, told her she doesn't have to go to church to go to Heaven. Through God's grace, Mary slowly adapted to the new me. I have to admit it was hard for her; she missed the man she fell in love with. I felt a sadness for her because I wanted her to be happy, but I couldn't return to the man I was. My heart and soul didn't want to go back to who I was. I had a new love in my life—the love of God. He didn't want me to replace my love for my wife, but to renew it. God wanted my love to be purified for my wife and everyone around me. My love was tainted and needed to be renewed, and this was what He was doing. He never abandoned us: He remained faithful to His word.

During the summer of that same year, I was still working for my twin brother, Philip. I remember his sending me on a service call to his parish's Catholic school to look at a hot water tank problem. My brother loved his church, and he did everything he could to help support the parish and the school, which included free labor at times. Father Anthony, who was the pastor at that church at the time of my conversion, met me at the door to let me into the school. I introduced myself to him, and we talked about Jesus for a little while. I have to admit I was probably too intense for him, maybe too judgmental. Father Anthony was good-natured and tolerated me. I think he had past experiences with "gung ho" Christians. Later down the road this meeting would serve a purpose.

I was very active at Christian Church, which continued operating out of the dance studio in Connecticut on Sunday mornings. There was always talk about starting a new church somewhere else, but it didn't happen while I was there. It did happen a couple of years later when they purchased a small Catholic Church that was for sale near a local dam. In the meantime, members of the church would meet at the dance studio on Saturday nights to set up chairs for Sunday morning services. On occasion, I would help them set up the chairs. Every Sunday before the services, I would meet the pastor's wife to get the keys for their vehicle to pick up and drop off parishioners who needed a ride so that they could attend.

I was in love with my new environment and my new friends. As they got to know me better, they would approach me to tell me about how impressed they were with my conversion. They also told me they had told others about me. Because they were so impressed with my experience, many would come to me and ask for advice. I began to grow in spiritual pride. It got to the point that even the pastor was asking me for advice. In my mind, I felt God was filling me with insight, and I was an instrument that God was using to save the world. I was so blinded by my spiritual pride, I was unable to see it. The devil has many ways of deceiving the soul without the soul having any knowledge of the deception. I couldn't see that, within my soul, I was dealing with a new kind of pride and self-love. Not the pride and self-love of the past which could be seen by the human eye. This one was more deadly to my soul because it couldn't be seen by the human eye. It was well disguised by my false humility. No matter what kind of pride we possess, it is still pride, and God hates pride. In time, God helped me see the errors of my ways, through my foolishness, my failures, and my sins. Even today, I struggle to achieve a more humble lifestyle, realizing the more humble I can become, the closer I can get to God. I find myself always on guard against the Devil. The Devil is very shrewd and can easily manipulate the mind without the mind ever knowing. Before you realize it, you're sinning, and have moved one step backward instead of forward. Every person on this earth has the opportunity to know God. You must always remember that the Devil will use everything in his power to keep you from the intimacy you can have with God. We can be blinded even when we think we're close to Him. Even today I am still somewhat blinded and weak in my intimacy with God.

Deaf Ears and God's Grace

Five more events happened to me that I can remember while I was attending Christian Church. One of them was when the pastor wanted to meet my parents. The pastor was a former Catholic and his mother is still a practicing Catholic today, as far as I know. I haven't seen the pastor or his wife for a couple of years. The pastor and I were really close friends, so I decided to have him meet my parents at their house. I gave my mother advanced notice, and we drove to their house where I introduced the pastor to my mother. My father was not around at the time. The three of us sat at my mother's kitchen table and she started the conversation with nothing special, definitely not a religious topic, to avoid a conflict. As the three of us continued talking at the table, the pastor decided to share his point of view with my mother that Mary, the Mother of God, was a sinner and had to repent. That was his perception of the Blessed Mother, which is very similar to what most Protestants think of Mary today. They believe the Blessed Mother was a sinner and had to repent, just as we all have to repent. They also believe that Mary was not a virgin and had children with Joseph. They don't view the Blessed Mother in the way a good Catholic should view her.

As the pastor continued talking to my mother, she sat there with a pleasant demeanor even though he was saying such negative things about our Blessed Mother. It saddens my heart that my Protestant brothers and sisters think so poorly of the Mother of God. During that particular part of the conversation, when the pastor was condemning our Blessed Mother, I drifted off. For some unknown reason I never heard a word of it, as if I were somewhere else, or in a place outside of their conversation. I can't describe it, or quite understand what really happened at that table. All I know is that, in my heart, I felt God didn't want me to hear that part of the conversation. It saddens me that any individual could think so little of the Blessed Mother who carried the son of God; a woman who would endure so much suffering for all humanity.

I never would have known about this conversation unless my mother told me about it a little while later. One day when I went to her house for coffee, she asked me, "Why didn't you say something when the pastor was talking about our Blessed Mother?" I explained that I never heard the conversation. She looked at me and said that she found it hard to believe that I never heard a word said against Mary, the Mother of God. Some of you might think I wasn't interested in the conversation—believe me I was. I wanted to make sure there would be no arguments, knowing that both my mother and the pastor held strong beliefs. I don't have an answer to this mystery, only my thoughts of what I think happened.

To some of you, I can say nothing that will make sense; to others, it will make all the sense in the world.

The second thing that happened to me was God's calling me back to the Catholic Church. When I told the pastor and his wife that I felt the Lord was calling me back to my Church, they told me they felt the Devil was deceiving me and I should reconsider. I was shocked and disappointed by their response, and I was angry because of their closed-mindedness, especially since the pastor was a former Catholic and, I believe, his mother is still a practicing Catholic. I've found in my journey that many Christians who have left the Catholic Church and have joined a Protestant church seem to carry with them a bitterness towards the Catholic Church.

The pastor also had a small prayer group that would meet one day each week for prayer and conversation. Shortly after the prayer meeting, the pastor and his wife asked me if I had time to talk with them alone in their car. I agreed, so we headed towards their car. The pastor and his wife sat in front and I sat in back. We were conversing back-and-forth about my decision to leave Christian Church. Suddenly, the strangest thing happened to me: while they were talking to me, my mind couldn't process what they were saying. Their mouths were moving but not a single word penetrated my mind. I heard them speaking, and knew words were coming from their mouths, but I was unable to process anything they were saying. I was looking right at them when they were speaking to me, and yet I felt blocked out of the conversation. I felt like my mind was in the clouds, far away from them, as if my body were there but my spirit wasn't. I was unable to comprehend what was going on. It was the strangest thing I've ever experienced. And, as they continued talking, I felt something inside me telling me it was time to leave. I looked at the pastor and his wife and told them there was something strange going on, because I couldn't process what they were saying to me and I would have to go. They looked at me as if I were crazy.

I got out of the car that night totally confused about what had just happened. I had never experienced anything like that before. It was not like the experience at my mother's house where I missed out on the conversation probably because I was more of a spectator and not a participant; it was different. I was in a car where I had two people looking directly at and talking to me, not as a spectator, but as a person engaged in the conversation. They were definitely two different kinds of experiences with one thing in common: in both experiences, the words spoken never entered my soul. Even today, I feel God didn't want me to hear what they had to say, and blocked my mind. These events happened months apart, but I put them together to present very similar events.

God's Voice

Before I go into the final three experiences, I'll try to explain them first because they happened within a short period of time—before I returned to the Catholic Church. I was near the end of the Bible, reading the "Book of Revelation." As I was reading in my bedroom, I was growing tired and decided to finish the next day. I closed the Bible, put it on my bureau, and went to bed. What I am about to tell you may seem difficult to believe—I would have found it hard to believe myself, before I came to know the Lord. I was falling to sleep, but hadn't yet reached a deep sleep. Ever since my conversion, I've tossed and turned while trying to fall asleep. When I was an alcoholic, I used to go to bed and pass right out. While in bed, I was awakened by a voice that filled the room. The voice was a strong voice that spoke with authority and power. Its tone had a gentle side to it, yet still firm. It was full of compassion, but spoke with conviction. I felt in my heart it was God speaking to me. The voice only said one word to me: "Obey." I remembered the voice was loud because it startled me before I could fall to sleep. I remember getting out of my bed, confused and afraid. I was unable to sleep so I opened up the Bible, got on top of the covers again, and continued reading the "Book of Revelation" from where I had left off.

I felt I was reading at a decent pace, considering I had just gotten out of bed. I was still a little shaken up, but I began to grow tired and, eventually, I started to slow down and nod off from being tired. As I was nodding off, I heard His voice again saying to me, "Obey." Again His voice startled me. I was exhausted and wanted to go back to sleep, but I was unable to because I was afraid. That night, I finished the "Book of Revelation" in a state of exhaustion. I went back to bed, exhausted, and finally fell asleep. The next day when I woke up, I wasn't sure if it had been a dream, or if it was real. Out of curiosity and my desire to know what had really happened that night, I decided to open the Bible. To my amazement, I found that my bookmark was at the last page of "Revelation." I realized that I had completed reading the Bible that night and that it hadn't been a dream.

To this day, and probably until the day I die, I will always remember the words of our Lord that were spoken to me that night. I've tried countless times to understand and to be obedient to His words as best I can. I've found in my journey that when I get discouraged or down on myself it's sometimes hard to be obedient to God and the prompting of the Holy Spirit. However when I'm strong in the spirit, I've found great joy and an inner peace in my life through my obedience. I was hesitant about sharing this part of my conversion only because it will be hard for many to believe. I feel obligated to share this truth regardless of the outcome. For us to deny the possibility that God could speak to an individual in this day and age would reject the love and power of God.

After eleven years, I'm still struggling with feeling in my heart that God should have chosen someone else to speak to, someone more educated or more faithful, anyone else besides me to do what He wills. There are so many other good people closer to God than I am. Why He chose an individual so sinful and weak in the English language to do his work is way beyond my own comprehension. I have given up trying to understand why God does what He does. I now accept whatever His plan is for me, uncertain of where I am going or what will be expected of me, trusting in Him and Him alone.

You Will be Alone

Another experience that happened to me at about the same time, occurred at Christian Church during one of their services. I believe it was late summer of that year but I'm not quite sure. In the front of the church, there was a little place where people could go to kneel, pray, or just to be alone. At that time, I was not sure what God was doing in my life. I still had doubts, fears, and was uncertain of the direction in which I was heading. I was also struggling with discerning what God's will was for me. While sitting in the second row of the church, something inside me moved me to go forward and kneel down so I could be alone to ask God for His guidance. While the music was playing and I was kneeling up front, all alone, and as I was trying to clear my mind and feel the presence of God inside my soul, I entered into some kind of interior peace. Then, out of nowhere, I received an interior communication that spoke to my soul. It said to me, "You will be alone." At first I was concerned because I felt confused and uncertain of the meaning of that message. I remember trying to figure out what it meant. My mind couldn't comprehend the meaning of being alone. At first I thought it meant that Mary and I were going to get a divorce and I would be all alone. So I said to the interior of my soul, "Am I getting divorced?" because that was the first thought that came to my mind. The voice didn't answer my question, and I remained silent waiting for Him to answer me. I was too young and weak in the spiritual sense to understand what alone meant.

Again, I heard the interior communication speak to my soul saying, "You will be alone." Again, I said to the interior of my soul, "Is my wife going to die and I will be alone?" Again, I waited for a response to my question and received no answer. I continued waiting for a response. The voice said a third time, "You will be alone." Again, I spoke to the interior of my soul asking, "Am I going to be without friends?" Again, I waited for a response to my question and received no answer. I don't remember everything I was thinking as I was trying to understand the meaning of, "You will be alone." All I remember is going back-and-forth with the interior communication eight times as it continued saying to me, "You will be alone." It never answered me. Finally, after hearing the interior communication eight times, I said to the Lord in the interior of my soul "Lord I do not know, nor do I understand what you mean by these words you have spoken to me, but I will do what you want from me."

I stood up and walked back to my seat, sat down, and as I was sitting the floodgates of my soul opened up and I burst into uncontrollable tears. There were people sitting all around me looking at me trying to figure out what was going on. I was unable to control my tears and continued to cry, unable to stop my emotions as they responded to the Lord's request. He touched my soul. My body, without knowledge of His presence, cried out tears of joy. I remember while I was crying uncontrollably, the pastor's wife turned around in shock, trying to understand what had just happened. It was very strange to me—usually people cry in response to the joy or the pain they're feeling through emotional or physical suffering. I had nothing on my mind—no reason to cry at all—I was just confused. I can't explain what happened to me. I know at that time, the meaning of being alone didn't register with me. All I can remember is crying uncontrollably with joy.

No one spoke to me after the service except for the pastor's wife, which was unusual for me because I always spoke to people after the service. She asked me what had happened, and I tried to explain it to her the best I could. How could I explain something I didn't understand myself? I told her I was tired and had to go. I left the church and I got into my car, trying to understand what the Lord had meant with his words to me about being alone. When I arrived home I shared my experience with my wife. She was concerned because she felt I was close to the Lord and that God was planning to take her from me so that I could do His purpose. She was thinking God would allow her to die so that I could continue doing more of His will, or that we would get divorced so I could be with a good Christian woman. Our minds, at times, are so limited to seeing God's will and purpose for us that we tend to think the worst, blinded by the truth in front of us.

13

The Interior Voice Continues and My Return to the Catholic Church

I remember receiving another interior communication, I believe within weeks of the previous experience that went something like this, "I want you to go to Mass at your brother Philip's church. There you will find they have an eight o'clock Mass and Father Anthony will be saying the Mass." As I mentioned earlier I met Father Anthony over the summer while working at the school, and we had only met once. I had no idea of the Mass schedule, or if Father Anthony was still at my brother's church.

I think within a week or two of that interior communication, I called the rectory of the church that Philip belonged to. I spoke with the secretary and asked her about their Mass schedule. I asked her if they had an eight o'clock Mass and she said, "Yes we do." When I asked her if she knew if Father Anthony would be saying the eight o'clock Mass, she replied, "No he's not scheduled for that Mass." I paused for a moment and asked her if she was sure, she said, "Yes, I'm sure." I have to admit I was a little disappointed and confused, but I knew what the interior communication had said, and I remember that God had said, "Obey," so I said to the Lord in my interior, "You said he'll be there, so I'll go."

Days before I attended the eight o'clock Mass, I received another interior communication that said, "Look past the failure of men and focus on the truth." When I received that communication, I asked myself, "What does that mean?" It made no sense to me at all. At the time of that communication, I was unable to interpret or understand its meaning. I was clueless, and didn't even know where to begin. Later in my spiritual journey, I would come to an understanding of that interior communication, but it wouldn't make sense until after being back in the Catholic Church for a little while.

Although the timing of these last three events could be off by a little—as I told you earlier they happened so close in proximity it's hard for me to pinpoint the exact timing—the events themselves are true and accurate as I have described them.

I call this my second awakening: I finally left my Protestant church and returned to the Catholic Church. I found myself no longer satisfied with what I call a "reduced ministry." I could no longer spend my life thinking that all I had to do was to accept Jesus as Lord and Savior to be saved and that I was also guaranteed a place in Heaven just because of this. I also struggled with the concept that those with other religious beliefs were condemned to Hell simply because they didn't accept Jesus as Lord and Savior. I was also troubled and saddened that my

Protestant brothers and sisters thought so little of the Blessed Mother who had endured so much suffering through her response to God.

I remember getting into my car and driving to Philip's church to attend the eight o'clock Mass. I entered the Church and sat down towards the front of the church, waiting patiently in the pew for the Mass to begin and for the arrival of the priest. When the priest came out to celebrate the Mass, my heart was filled with joy and amazement—it was Father Anthony. I was somewhat shocked and, at the same time, very excited. I was in seventh heaven during the entire Mass. I can't describe the joy I felt, because the Lord fulfilled His promise. I found out later that at the last minute the other priest who was to have celebrated the Mass was unable to make it, and Father Anthony had to cover for him. After hearing that, my soul leaped again for joy. I knew the interior communication was true, because God at the last minute made it all happen. I also felt in my heart that God brought me back home to the true Church of Jesus Christ.

I know the Catholic Church has undergone many trials, and many people have experienced heartache because of the corruption that the Church has gone through throughout the many years of its existence. We need to know and understand that this is because of a failure in the human nature of our spiritual leaders. I don't defend or condone these actions because I understand my own weaknesses and frailties. I have also come to realize that our Church has many avenues towards achieving a deeper relationship with God. It is through these avenues such as the Eucharist, adoration, confession, and the rosary that I have journeyed deeper than I could have ever expected. A lot of our faith is misunderstood and misused. Many Catholics fail by not trying to understand the many avenues available through the Catholic Church. Many have gone through the traditions and routines of the Mass without embracing the true source of God's love and mercy for us. I don't stand in judgment of anyone, and I don't elevate myself above anyone; I simply know in my heart that anyone can achieve the joy necessary; but it means we must trust in God. We need to let go of ourselves, go to Him, and use the avenues of the Church that God has provided for us.

14

Called to Serve Him and a New Voice

God's timing is perfect—that same weekend the lector at the Mass I attended made an announcement that the Church was looking for lectors and Eucharistic ministers. When the lector made that announcement, my soul filled with such joy, that it was rejoicing beyond what any words could describe. I knew God was calling me to be a lector and Eucharistic minister. There was no doubt in my mind. I tried to wait patiently for the Mass to end, but I was so excited that I was like a child waiting for a present. After Mass, I hurried to meet the lector who said she would be at the back of the church for anyone interested in signing up. I met with the lector and introduced myself. She probably thought that I was strange because I had a smile on my face from ear-to-ear. I told her that I wanted to sign up for both lector and Eucharistic minister. She said, "That's great." After I signed up, I left the church filled with such joy. I remained in that joy while driving to my parents' house to tell them the good news.

The first person I thought of was my mother, because my mother was very excited that I had returned to the Catholic Church. She told me that she knew deep in her heart that God would not abandon her or her prayers. When I arrived at my parents' house to share the great news, I knocked at the door, went inside and sat at the kitchen table where my mother was sitting. I told my mother I had signed up to be a lector and a Eucharistic minister at my church. My mother looked me in the eye and said to me, "Oh no, Son, you can't be a lector because you mumble. You've mumbled all your life." My heart was saddened when I heard those words come from my mother's mouth. In my heart I knew she was correct—I had mumbled all my life. She always felt I was too lazy to open my mouth to speak, and maybe I was. But the joy I felt was too strong and too convincing for me to give in to my mother's words—there was no doubt in my mind that it was the Holy Spirit calling me to do God's work. I love my mother and I will always respect her, but the spirit was too strong and it was driving me with an intense force. I couldn't fight it, nor resist it. I would have to trust in the Lord, certain that He would not abandon me.

It might be hard for those who lack knowledge of spiritual things to understand that good Christians can be used by the Devil to interfere or act as a wedge between God and the one he calls to do His will. I believe in that moment in time my mother failed to look at God's calling me to do His will, and only saw my human inability to do His will. A mother who loves her children wants to protect them from humiliation. My mother in that moment was just trying to do that. In our journey, we all have moments of doubt. This is our failure. It denies us that deeper intimacy with Jesus Christ, our Lord and Savior, creating larger voids of emptiness within us.

I am not sure which Mass I first lectored at—I believe it was the eight o'clock. I was nervous because I'd never spoken in public and I knew I mumbled. I wasn't really a good reader, considering that at the time the only book I had read was the Bible. I felt the Lord had prepared me for this moment and I had to put my best into it, so I practiced the readings almost every night for a month. I was still filled with fear and doubt because I'm human and I had a clear understanding of what I was capable of doing regarding my mumbling. In my heart, I knew the Lord would be there with me the whole time, but I was doubting Him.

I was at the podium about to speak my first word as a lector from Scriptures, when an inner peace came upon me. The Holy Spirit opened my mouth, I began to speak, and, to my own amazement, my voice flowed at a perfect pace—not too fast, and not too slow. My voice was clear so that the congregation could hear it and understand me. My voice changed as well. It had a new tone which is hard to describe. I felt like I had the voice of an evangelist, full of emotion. A voice that spoke with authority, compassion, and love. I felt like I had the voice of the Evangelist, himself. I stood at the podium in total amazement.

After lectoring a few times, I fell deeper into spiritual pride. Most of my life consisted of insecurities, never feeling like anybody special. Even when some people did praise me for my accomplishments—when I weight lifted and played softball—it still left me feeling empty. It felt different this time because I was working for the Lord, and not myself. I felt loved and dear to Him as if I were special. The Devil took his opportunity because I felt special, and I began to think I was above everyone else. I became inflated with spiritual pride because people were amazed by what God did in my life. In time, God would show me the errors of my ways. I still lector today at a church in Massachusetts. I know in my heart it is not my voice. I don't wish to boast—it is the voice of the Holy Spirit speaking through my mouth. It is a voice that cannot be duplicated. It is not like acting and rehearsing lines—it's totally different. Some people might think it's the same thing, but trust me, it's not. I have no acting skills and a poor memory. I'll never be able to describe what passes through my mouth when I speak. All I know is, it's not me. I want to give the glory to the true source that deserves the glory. I take no credit, and praise God for the voice He has given to me.

It was time to find a spiritual director. Father Anthony became my first spiritual director. God knew what He was doing because Father Anthony was very charismatic. My conversion would require a charismatic individual that could help me understand what I was going through and would continue to go through. Father Anthony was perfect for this because he understood and guided me through my spiritual growth.

God Calls Us to Forgive

When I was at Christian Church, the Lord was doing powerful things in me as I described earlier. Unfortunately, the pastor and I were not on good terms when I left his Church. I felt he was angry with me because I returned to the Catholic Church, but I knew I could no longer remain there. There are many lapsed Catholics who carry a bitterness with them towards the Church. They also believe that the Church has too many man-made rules. I felt the pastor felt this way about the Catholic Church because he was a former Catholic who had left the Church. The Lord doesn't want Christians to feel bitterness and hatred towards each other because of our lack of understanding each other. I love my Protestant brothers and sisters, and always will, because in their own unique way they have a love for the Lord and engage in fellowship with each other because of their love for Christ. It was that love for Jesus that, as time went on, called me through the Spirit to talk to my former pastor to try to make things right with him.

One day, while driving by Christian Church about a year or two later, I saw the pastor's vehicle out in front. I was moved to pull into the parking lot. At first, he seemed shocked to see me. I said hello to him and to his wife who was with him. I asked him if he had a moment, which he said he did, so I decided to sit down outside on the steps of his church to talk with him. I began telling the pastor about how I had felt when I left his church: the anger, the betrayal, and the emptiness because of his rejection of my returning to the Catholic Church. The pastor told me that he felt that the Devil had deceived me and convinced me to leave his church. He also said that he was concerned that when I left his church, I was going to take a lot of his followers with me. He said this was because the spirit inside me was so strong that it drew people to me. In that moment, spiritual pride filled my soul: I felt joy in my soul, but the joy I felt was a prideful joy. My soul appeared to me to be complete because I perceived this to be some kind of victory, and yet without true understanding I still remained far from the Lord. I am not repeating the pastor's words so I can boast, but to give you an understanding of what was going on in my life at that time. I believe the same spirit that entered me in my conversion remains with me to the present day.

Spiritual Direction, God's Grace and the Dream

I met with Father Anthony on several occasions for spiritual direction. Father Anthony was familiar with this spirit that was inside me. There was one occasion, very early in my return to the Catholic Church, that I was talking to him about the Bible and my interpretation of certain Scriptures. I told him when I read Scriptures they seemed to have a deeper meaning beyond the surface. I also told him that they were filled with many emotions that pierced my soul. Father Anthony asked me to explain what I meant, so I did. I shared with him a certain verse from the Bible and began to explain the deeper understanding I drew from it. When I finished explaining my concept of the verse, he looked at me and was obviously filled with great joy and amazement because of what the Holy Spirit was doing within me. On a couple of occasions, he said to me, "You are growing in leaps and bounds." The Lord was giving me some insight and understanding of the Scriptures—not in an intellectual sense, but in the spiritual understanding, in its simplicity. Believe me, I'm far from being an intellect according to the world's definition of an intellect.

What I am trying to describe to you is my understanding of how to achieve a deeper union with God, not through the intellect, but through His spirit. I can attest to my ignorance in the world of intellects because I'm far from being well educated in theology and philosophy. And yet, the things of God seemed to make sense to me, which has allowed me to live an interior life outside of my selfish desires. I tried to fight my selfish nature, and continue searching for Him on the road to humility. I don't have all of the answers, and I am not even sure if I have any of the answers. I only share the insight that I have received and have come to understand from reading a few books of the great Saints and the Bible. But most of the insight I've received, I believe, came to me at the Chapel of the Blessed Sacrament through prayer and discernment. I feel blessed that God has allowed me to be part of something so awesome. I have come to God in my nothingness, and in my nothingness God can do great things. In myself, I can do nothing. I've seen that through grace alone, which I call the accelerant, I can do all things. I call grace the accelerant, because it's a gift from God that works with the fire of the Holy Spirit, causing a spiritual ignition inside my soul, burning with an intensity for the Lord. It allows me to move beyond the natural state into the supernatural state.

I remember on one occasion, while still under the spiritual direction of Father Anthony, I was at home in bed, sleeping. I had a dream, and in this dream I was standing about knee high in water in a very small pond. As I was looking across the pond about fifteen to twenty feet away from me, a snake launched out of the water, straight at me, and bit me on my left hand. When I woke from the dream, I looked at my left hand and to my amazement saw two impressions on my left hand that looked like snake bite marks. These impressions lasted for about three days. I showed my wife Mary the marks, and told her about the dream. She looked at my hand in total shock. After we tried to understand the meaning of the marks and the dream, a thought came to my head, and I then realized the reality of the supernatural and the natural world existing together at the same point in time. As crazy as this sounds, I believe the demonic realm is very real and dwells in our world with us—that demons and angels are among us. Spiritual warfare is a reality and the physical body can be affected in this battle. I talked to my spiritual director about this because I was concerned about the dream. He reminded me about a certain Scripture passage from the Book of Numbers that spoke about a bronze serpent that Moses mounted on a pole and, whenever anyone who had been bitten by a serpent looked at the bronze serpent, he recovered. He also told me about how paramedics have this symbol on the sleeves of their shirts. He said that this could be a good thing, and I shouldn't worry. Father Anthony and I spent a lot of time trying to figure out its meaning, but were unsuccessful. We both had our own ideas about this dream, but were unable to come up with a concrete answer.

On another occasion, while in confession, I was telling Father Anthony about a situation where there seemed to be no hope for a person I knew. I felt that this person would perish because of their sinful lifestyle. Father Anthony said to me, "You can never sin against hope," and to this day his comment remains in my heart. At first I didn't quite understand its meaning, but then it made all of the sense in the world. I realized I shouldn't deny hope because I also had appeared to be hopeless to a lot of Christians before my own conversion. The person I saw appeared to me to have no hope, but I realized that person was what I used to be. I appeared to be hopeless in the eyes of many, and now I'm an example of hope to others who may be lost and have gone astray. God's mercy is the hope for everyone—there is no one on this earth who is without hope in Jesus Christ, our Lord and Savior.

Prayer Groups

When I was still attending the church in Connecticut I joined a prayer group. It wasn't a very large one; there were just four of us. The others in the prayer group always waited for me to speak because every time I spoke, God was filling my mouth with such profound insight. For me, the downside of this was that my head was becoming filled with spiritual pride. I'm not sure if I was blind to it, or if I was enjoying the attention I was receiving. I was on a spiritual high and I didn't give it a thought. It got to the point where two members made a CD cover and gave it to me, asking me to speak about spiritual warfare. At first, I was flattered, but deep inside my soul I knew I couldn't do this unless the Spirit spoke through me. It said on the cover, "The Battle for Your Soul with David Saul." The two individuals felt that the Holy Spirit was strong inside me, and insisted that I speak on that topic. I said I would see what I could do, because part of me knew who I really was. I still lacked the confidence necessary for this task because I was still too weak in the spirit. I still have the CD cover. My constant reminder of the two individuals who believed in me, and in that fire that burned so strongly inside my soul—a fire that should never be quenched.

I enjoyed the prayer group and the people in it. They were very supportive of me and my conversion back to the Catholic Church. Eventually the group split up due to a lack of interest, or possibly doubts of other people's spiritual gifts. I feel the problem with prayer groups and other religious groups is people's lack of humility. People's pride always gets in the way of God's work, creating doubt and a lack of understanding of God's spiritual gifts. God has many spiritual gifts and distributes them as He pleases; however we sometimes think we're the only ones who receive the gifts. I remember for many years doubting and being jealous of other people and their gifts. In time, God taught me that we must try to unite our gifts in the hope of reaching many who might be lost and confused. What might appear to us as strange or abnormal is actually normal in the spiritual world, and our lack of understanding moves us to ignorance of the beauty of these gifts. I have learned to appreciate others and the gifts God has given them. Who could know better than God? Eventually, those in our group did their own thing because the problem was in our individual personalities and our spiritual weakness. How often we tend to forget that it's about doing God's work and not our own agenda. Our human weaknesses will always get in the way of truly being what God calls us to be.

18

Adoration Chapel

The Holy Spirit was now calling me to join the adoration chapel in Connecticut. One day, I decided to sign up for one hour a week. I think it was on a Tuesday night from five o'clock to six o'clock in the evening. That lasted a little while before I decided to move to Friday night from seven to eight p.m. Slowly I kept adding one hour to my Friday night and over time I eventually was doing five hours straight, from seven to midnight. I have to admit, at first I found the Chapel to be a chore and I didn't like it. In the winter I watched the weather in hopes of a snowstorm on my assigned night and was very happy when they canceled adoration because of bad weather. Often times I found adoration boring and time passed slowly by. I realize today, the reason I didn't like the Chapel at first was because I was still self-absorbed. I still had a great deal of spiritual pride and lacked humility. I had no prayer life, and prayer was a drudgery. I felt, even though the Holy Spirit was guiding me and filling me with insight, I still lacked intimacy with God. I was existing in self, and the love of self. I loved all the praise and attention I was getting from people and I was very prideful. I boasted to other people about the hours I did on Friday nights. I did adoration for all the wrong reasons. Eventually my spiritual director, Father Anthony, found out about my boasting and questioned my intentions. I reassured him that I wasn't boasting; I loved the chapel. I lied to him because I was ashamed of myself and didn't want to tell him the truth. I wanted him to think I was holy. I was a changed man, but far from perfect. There would be things I needed to learn the hard way because it would be the only way I would see past my pride. People think that when you're converted you're supposed to be perfect. And sometimes you have to pretend to be someone that you eventually will become. People expect so much from you when you go through a conversion; they look to you as a beacon of hope. I didn't want to let anyone down—they believed in me—but at times it was difficult to meet their expectations because of my human frailties. They didn't realize I was still new to the many ways of God. Still a child wants so much to learn. I was carrying with me a lifetime of memories of a sinful man, blinded by the many errors of my ways. I was converted, but I was not purified. It would only be through my trials and sufferings that God would purify my pride within me because pride does evil things. It takes control of your heart, mind, soul, and body. It leaves you in a world of sin, broken and confused, empty of the good things of the Lord. I know now that if I want to achieve a deeper intimacy with God, it can only be achieved through true humility.

Even though I had signed up for five hours for the wrong reasons, God allowed me to learn from this. I wanted people in church to think that I was holy. I know I did it for the wrong reasons, but it still served a purpose. It was in those five hours that God enlightened me to the suffering of his son, Jesus Christ, in the garden of Gethsemane. I never would have understood His suffering unless I had spent those five hours in the Chapel on a Friday night. It was during those long five hours that took their toll on me—there were many nights where I was totally exhausted. Sometimes I would lie on the floor between the crucifix and the altar and just fall asleep; other times I would stare at the clock waiting for it to end. Then one night God opened my eyes and I realized that Jesus was giving me a glimpse of understanding how He felt that night in the garden. I realized how exhausted He was, and how much more He would have to endure without food or drink. We can never truly understand the suffering Jesus went through, nor the amount of love it took for His sacrifice on the cross.

After that, I dropped my hours down to one and no longer remained a captain of the nine o'clock hour. I lost my desire when I came to the realization that I was going to the chapel for the wrong reasons. I felt ashamed and foolish, and guilt flooded my soul. I just wanted to hide where no one could find me. You, Oh Lord, deserved my praise, and I gave you a cup filled with my pride. I was a miserable servant, deserving nothing, and you showed me mercy. I was blind, and you opened my eyes. My mouth spoke empty words, and you gave them life. I eventually left the chapel in Connecticut and started attending the chapel in Massachusetts where no one knew me. I wanted to start all over again, and to do it for the right reasons. I'm telling you this so that if you ever decide to sign up for an hour at the chapel, you'll do it for the benefit of your soul. I encourage everyone to do one hour a week at the chapel as a minimum but to do it for the right reasons. Do it to be alone with the Lord in prayer or through spiritual reading. If you do it for the right reasons, you'll get the benefits of the true joy that God intended for all of us. I learned a lot through my mistakes—which I had to make. If I had never made those mistakes, how would the Lord have taught me the error of my ways? The Lord, in His mercy, took the bad and turned it into something good. For this, I will be forever grateful. There are no words of thanks that will ever be enough.

I spent a few years at the chapel in Connecticut and had some great experiences there. I'll share a few of them with you. This next experience couldn't have happened unless I had engaged in gossiping. It came to my attention that a certain priest didn't believe in one of the Church's teachings. If the customer I was talking to hadn't told me about him, I never would've known; however, the information she gave me would be necessary for my encounter with him. We all know that gossiping is wrong, and most of us tend to engage in it—it's one of our human weaknesses. Did God, knowing my weakness, use my sin of gossiping and turn it into something good? I know that gossiping can be dangerous, but sometimes we feel we have something important to share. However, oftentimes we discredit an individual's name. I know that certain people gossip too much, but some only gossip a little. Regardless of who we are, young or old, we somehow enter into gossiping—whether we start the gossip, or get dragged into it. The next experience will give you something to think about.

One day, while talking to a customer at her house, I was told about a priest from a church in Connecticut who didn't believe in Purgatory. I was surprised. This would be the first time I would understand what God meant when he said to me, "Look past the failure of men and focus on the truth." We have a tendency to come to our own understanding of what God's words mean. It's one of the reasons we have so many different religions and beliefs. However a Catholic priest is responsible for being obedient to the Church's teachings, and must not form his own interpretation of the Church's teachings. Unfortunately, there are those priests who don't follow the Church's teachings, resulting in chaos and confusion. This often causes parishioner's questioning of the Church's teachings.

One night when I was sitting in the back of the chapel, this priest came in and sat in the back right next to me. He didn't know me because I wasn't a parishioner at his church. I was nervous, but felt compelled to say something to him. I said to him, "I heard that you don't believe in Purgatory." He seemed calm, waiting for my next remark. I didn't think he was concerned that I knew because many of his parishioners also knew. We began to converse about the matter, point-counterpoint. He said to me, "What about the sinner on the cross who repented of his sinfulness? Jesus forgave him and said to the sinner in return, 'This day you will be with me in paradise.'" I have to admit, that was a tough one. After pondering this, I explained to the priest that when we leave this world of time, we enter a timeless world, and, if that is correct, the sinner could spend time in Purgatory and still go to Heaven on that same day because that day will never end. He seemed surprised by my answer, and we continued to share our thoughts with each other. We eventually said our goodbyes without my knowing if the conversation was a waste of time or not.

The same priest came back to the chapel a second time, sat down next to me again, and we again conversed. In my closing argument, I said to him, "If what the great saints have revealed to us about Purgatory is not true, then the great saints are liars." I felt he'd have to make a choice: did he believe in the private revelation of the great saints, or not? If not, he would be calling them liars. All of us have the same choice: whether we're going to believe these private revelations, or not. I know in my heart that the great saints have a deeper intimacy with Christ than we do, and what they have revealed to us I believe to be true. We ended our conversation that night on good terms.

I found out a week or two later from a parishioner of his church that the priest spoke during Mass about Purgatory. The parishioner I talked with was surprised because she said he never spoke about Purgatory because he didn't believe in it. I don't know today if that priest believes in Purgatory, or not. It's possible to that he spoke about Purgatory to quiet down his parish. I can only hope and pray that he believes in what the Church teaches. I know a lot of Christians—Catholics and Protestants—who believe in what they want to believe. I encourage Catholics to try to learn and understand the teachings of the Church and why we have them. I'm always trying to understand the deeper meaning of the Church's teachings and have found them to be beneficial to my spiritual growth.

I met my friend Anne at the chapel one Friday night. I always sat in the back of the chapel, probably because they had the most comfortable chairs in the back. During the time I've spent at the chapel, I have seen a lot of people come in, spend a little time, then leave. One Friday night, Anne walked into the chapel. It was the first time I'd ever seen her there. She came in, genuflected to our Lord at the altar, and knelt down on a kneeler in the front of the chapel. I thought nothing of it. She began to pray as if she were pleading with the Lord, asking for His help and guidance, and upon her shoulders she appeared to be carrying so much suffering and hardship. Without our knowledge, God was listening to both of us, answering our prayers at the same time, arranging everything for our encounter. Anne knelt and prayed for almost forty-five minutes. During that time, I was receiving what I call the interior communications. I received three of these, telling me to go and talk to this woman. I always waited for at least three of these communications, just to be sure it wasn't my conscience speaking. I wasn't really familiar enough with these communications yet to understand the deeper purpose of them, and was still hesitant in responding to them. Usually our pride keeps us from responding to them because we feel we might embarrass ourselves. This is a natural response of the flesh and not of the spirit.

I walked up to Anne and introduced myself. We were able to share a little with each other, but I can't completely remember the conversation. When Anne departed, I really didn't think much about it. Anne came in on a couple of other occasions on Friday nights while I was at the chapel. I wasn't moved to talk to her, so I left her alone to pray. As I was sitting there, I felt a tugging, or an attraction, to her—not a physical attraction—it was something totally unfamiliar to me. The spirit within me was being drawn to her, not knowing why. Then it seemed like she disappeared for a couple of months or so. I felt a connection to her, some kind of attraction or need for this person—it's hard to describe what I felt. I know it was not like falling in love, because I felt no physical attraction. It was like some kind of glue that was binding me to her—it wasn't natural, but supernatural.

Book 4

Called to Imitate Christ Through the Church

1

A Different Kind of Friendship

We became very close friends. God put us together to build upon each other spiritually because we both were lacking certain things necessary for our spiritual growth. I was still lacking a prayer life and Anne was lacking understanding of the things of God. We were like building blocks, building upon each other's strengths. Through Anne, I learned how to develop a deeper intimacy with God through my prayer life. I saw Anne's prayer life and wanted the intensity that Anne had possessed. And Anne, through conversing with me, came to a greater understanding of the things of God and established a deeper union with Him through what He taught me. I believe that God puts people into our lives so we can learn something from them for our spiritual growth.

I have to admit this new friendship was troubling me—I knew I wasn't in love with Anne, but I couldn't shake myself free from feeling connected to her. So one day, while sitting at the kitchen table, my heart was deeply troubled, I asked the Lord to give me an understanding of what was going on. On March 10, 2013 I received an interior communication at a rapid rate that lasted less than a minute. As I was sitting at the table, I noticed a pen and a piece of paper in front of me. This enabled me to record the communication on paper and save what was revealed to me. The interior communication said, "The relationship is supernatural, omitting sensations of the natural relationship, working in the elevation of each soul supernaturally for the growth of the soul for the greater union with God through the natural bodies: natural emotions working to move into supernatural nature. Only through the weakening of the natural can the supernatural be weakened. Through grace, the natural is suppressed and the supernatural elevated. The relationship exists in a supernatural state in total love and union with God." As I received this communication I understood it as I was writing it down. Finally, I had an answer and a understanding of what I felt. I felt a freedom that day because the Lord gave me an understanding of this friendship. I now knew the connection that I felt was in the supernatural, and I realize today that, through Anne, God taught me how to pray and many other things, such as compassion and mercy.

Anne and I attended many church and religious events together. We would also talk on the phone for hours about the things of God and sometimes about the things that troubled us in our lives. We tried to offer each other advice in the hope of helping each other understand the trials that we were going through. Some people think that if you mention someone's name, you're gossiping. I feel that sometimes, if you're having a problem with a certain individual, you need to mention their name so that the other person can offer you advice. On occasion, people's names who were part of Anne's and my lives would come up in our conversations. We would try to offer each other advice in the hope of remedying the problem. However, we tried to be very cautious about not entering into gossip because of our knowledge of how destructive gossip can be to a person and to our souls. As Christians, we should be more aware of our conversations with others, consciously trying to avoid gossip since it's so easy to drift into it.

Eventually, Anne and I desired to know more about the things of God. In our journey to go deeper, we still maintained a balanced lifestyle so that we didn't neglect our responsibilities to our family. When I needed to talk about the things of God, I could always rely on Anne. Anne and I differed in personalities—I tend to consider myself more emotionally sentimental. Our friendship was a friendship based in the spiritual. I will always encourage spiritual friendships, because they're built upon Christ as the foundation, helping two individuals to grow stronger in the things of God. However, because I am more sensitive, I felt a need for more security in the emotional side of our friendship. Because of that need, I would occasionally fall into the emotional side of my personality, not neglecting the spiritual, but feeling the need for emotional support in our friendship: the need for a friend just for the sake of having someone to talk to and do things with. Emotional friendships rely on a foundation that can be unstable at times. Things can be misinterpreted or misunderstood, causing friction between two individuals. It's now my opinion that we should always maintain spiritual friendships and become less dependent on the emotional side of friendships.

In my journey, I have seen people neglect their families because they misunderstand what God wants from them. Sometimes, because we let our emotions interfere with spiritual reasoning, we tend to deceive ourselves into thinking we're doing the things of God, but because of our lack of understanding and maturity in the spirit, we feed into our flesh instead. But God, in His great wisdom, watching me travel in and out of spiritual and emotional friendships, slowly put an end to the time Anne and I spent together. This allowed me to refocus on my spiritual friendship and also my relationship with my spouse so that she might not feel neglected, even though, in my mind, she wasn't. He allowed things to come up, allowing our plans to fall by the wayside. At first, this troubled me because I enjoyed Anne's friendship and spending time with her. I had no one else I could really share the depth of my soul with. In time, I realized what the Lord was doing—he was drawing me back to Himself as it should be. Don't get me wrong—friendships are good—but we should never be dependent on anyone more than our dependency on God. Always remember, friends can let you down, not just once but more often than we think. We're all frail and selfish to some degree and need to understand our imperfections. Our imperfections keep us from loving others as God loves us. God will never let you down. I've come to realize this. Over time, I've realized that I can't put my trust in people. Not that I can't trust people, because certain people are trustworthy, but we're all human. We're unable to let go of ourselves completely, because of self-love; only God's grace can help us love as the great Saints loved. In order to love others, we have to love God first with all of our heart, body, mind, and soul. If God becomes the center point of our lives, then everything branches off that center point. God is perfect love. Try to make God your center point. Any other center point will lead you away from embracing God's love completely. Anne and I still stay in contact with each other to discuss religion and faith. But it will never be like it was. As it should be.

Remaining Obedient to the Interior Communication

I will share one more incident which occurred at the chapel. It was on a Saturday afternoon. Anne was unable to make it to the chapel that day, so she called me and asked me to cover for her, which I did. I was sitting in the back, as I always did in prayer and silence. At one point, three young men walked in and sat together in front, a couple of seats apart from each other. I thought nothing of it, and continued with my prayers. As I was sitting in prayer, I began to receive interior communications telling me there was a seminarian in my presence. I never respond to the first communication—I always wait for a second or third communication before I respond. Finally, after the third communication, one of the young men who was sitting on the outside of the row turned around. I looked him in the eye and asked if there was a seminarian present. At this, the other two young men turned around and looked at me for a brief moment and then affirmed that the young man in the middle was a seminarian. They looked at me, wondering how I knew. I explained to them that the Holy Spirit sometimes communicates with me without rhyme or reason, and that I try to respond to His prompting as best I can.

I tried to explain to them how the Holy Spirit can work in certain individuals, realizing I was still ignorant in my complete understanding of the Spirit. I became friendly over time, with one of the young men named Isaiah; I still remain in contact with him today. On occasion, I share with him what the Spirit reveals to me. I told him that his friend, the seminarian, would drop out of the seminary—that the Lord had said he would not complete his course. Isaiah looked at me in surprise, but in time the prophecy did come true and Isaiah told me a couple of months later that his friend dropped out of the seminary. I share a lot with Isaiah as the Spirit shares with me in the hope that Isaiah will establish a deeper interior life and find true joy through Jesus.

Today Isaiah is studying to become a priest. I hope and pray he will succeed. I have to admit that within him I saw some of the motives that drove him to this decision. Though his motives are honorable, I feel in my heart they are not the right ones, nor strong enough to maintain what is required of a great priest. I also feel that Isaiah won't complete the priesthood unless the three things of the flesh that I revealed to him are removed by God's grace. Our flesh sometimes can be stronger than our motives. Our motives deceive us in what God truly calls us to be. Sometimes people enter the priesthood for the wrong reasons. It was before I returned to the Catholic Church that the Lord gave me the three understandings of why an individual would enter the priesthood. Only one of the three reasons is true to the call of God. The two other reasons are security and power which are formed out of the distortion in a man thinking of the priesthood. I wish not to comment on the other two reasons. I can only encourage anyone who would consider the vocation of priesthood to be true to God and His Word.

Receiving the Eucharist Not in a State of Grace

I would like to write about some of my Eucharistic experiences in the Catholic Church. I have to admit I didn't fully understand the Church's teachings about Holy Communion. I tried to understand through Holy Scriptures and other sources, and I spent four months trying to understand the truer and deeper meaning of Communion with Jesus through receiving the Eucharist. After four months, I still doubted Jesus's presence in the Eucharist. At the time, it seemed too much for me to understand and make sense of. I remember reading St. Paul in Holy Scriptures in the Book of Corinthians when he wrote about, "those who eat this bread unworthily bring a judgment upon themselves." I'm not a theologian; I am only sharing with you what I have come to understand about this passage. If the Eucharist isn't real, then how can there be a judgment against anyone. In other words, reading these words symbolically wouldn't make any sense at all. There can be no judgment if it were simply symbolic. Also, St. Paul writes about the Real Presence of Jesus in the Eucharist. He writes about defilement against an individual who consumes the bread unworthily. I perceive "unworthily" as not being in a state of grace. It made sense in the intellect, but it wasn't enough for me, I needed more to believe.

My first understanding of the reality of Jesus's presence in the Eucharist happened at Mass months after my return to the Catholic Church. I was a Eucharistic minister at the time, and my wife, Mary, was attending Mass occasionally just to keep me happy. In my conversion, her lifestyle wasn't really affected—she didn't change much. She was still stuck in our old lifestyle. She wasn't in a state of grace according to the Church's teachings because she hadn't gone to confession in years—since she was a child. I'm not saying this in judgment, but with an understanding of what the Church teaches about being in grace. Mary was in line at this Mass, waiting to receiving Communion from me. When Mary reached the front of the line, ready to receive Communion, I was moved to say to her, "Behold the Lamb of God," instead of saying to her, "The body of Christ." I placed the Eucharist gently in her hands, as I do with everyone who comes to me for Communion, and right before our eyes we watched the Eucharist fly out of her hands straight up about two feet into the air and then land on the ground at our feet. We both looked at each other in shock. Mary then picked up the Eucharist and consumed it because I was still in shock. I realized in that moment of time, God was showing me how He was being defiled by a soul not in a state of grace. I cannot emphasize enough that the defilement is not Mary only, but all those who consume the Eucharist in great sin. I believe that the Eucharist works with a soul that is in the state of grace. I also believe that a soul that is not in the state of grace renders the Eucharist powerless. The soul becomes a mirror that reflects the presence of our Lord away from the soul. Therefore, the soul is unworthy to receive our Lord because the mirror hides the darkened soul behind it. It's through Confession that the soul enters the state of grace which is necessary to receive Jesus worthily. Through the Eucharist and a true contrition through confessions, the soul can achieve a deeper union and intimacy with God. I encourage everyone to make an attempt to research and understand the miracles of the Eucharist and the power of Confession. Through these avenues and the many others that the Catholic Church provides, you can achieve the joy of the Lord. There is nothing in this world that can compare to the joy and peace that you will experience through the joy of the Lord. It also brings hope in the resurrection, allowing us to spend eternity in the next life with our Lord and Savior, Jesus Christ.

A Taste of True Joy in Union with Jesus

I mentioned the joy of the Lord, so let me share the maximum experience I had in a state that I can't describe. I was still having doubts, as most of us do, about the Eucharist. So many people say that they believe in the Real Presence of Jesus in the Eucharist, but deep down in their hearts they're saying "no," and their intellect is saying "yes." I remember reading in the Bible a passage about a man asking Jesus to help him with his unbelief. I felt like that man who needed Jesus's help. He wasn't the only one struggling with unbelief, I was also struggling with unbelief. One day, I was standing in the Communion line at Mass, waiting to receive Communion, pondering both my unbelief and the unbelief of the man in Scriptures. As I was in line drawing closer to receive Communion, I asked the Lord to help me with my unbelief; then I reached the priest. Right before receiving, I asked the Lord again to help me with my unbelief. I held out my hands and the priest placed the Eucharist in them. I picked it up and consumed it. Immediately after consuming the Eucharist I felt this intense joy flood my soul. I tried to contain it, but was unable to and, as I was walking back to my seat, I began to smile ear-to-ear, unable to wipe the grin off of my face. I got back to my pew and sat down. My wife looked at me and asked me what was wrong. I looked at her, still smiling ear-to-ear, unable to describe to her what I was feeling. I was filled with great joy and an inner peace. This lasted almost three hours.

After Mass, we left the church and went to a restaurant where my daughter, Ruth, was working. I remember sitting down at a table with my wife and seeing a person at another table that I really disliked. I remember looking at him, unable to feel any hatred or bitterness towards him. I was unable to feel anything that wasn't love. You could have put my worst enemy in front of me and I would have been unable to feel anything other than love, itself. God allowed me to experience those three hours in total joy with Him. I've never felt that kind of intense joy and love again in my life to this day. I wonder now if for those three hours God had allowed me a taste of Heaven. I was immersed in true love, and I was love. Love in the purest form; it wasn't selfish. I never saw myself—my needs didn't exist. I could only see the needs of others, and I wanted to satisfy their needs, which I did. Part of me is saddened that I couldn't stay in that state. I realize that I will probably only achieve that state again in Heaven. I'm happy that the Lord allowed me to experience three hours of Heaven, and I look forward to going to Heaven, if I'm found worthy. I'm hoping and praying that I can experience a lifetime in that joy.

The Blood of Christ is Real Drink

My final and most powerful experience came several years later. God's timing is always perfect. My neighbors who live across the street from me invited me to their house to converse with them and to try a new kind of wine. They liked wine and would experiment with different varieties. When they invited me, I was outside for some reason. In all the years I've known them, they had never invited me to try their wine, even prior to my conversion. So I decided to go over and sample their wine. I sat at the kitchen table, waiting for the shot glass of wine that soon arrived. I asked them the contents of the alcohol which they told me and I remember it being between twelve and fifteen percent alcohol. Strangely enough, I believe that the wine used by Catholic Church during the Consecration is about the same percentage of alcohol. I thought nothing about taking a sip of wine since it had been several years since I last drank. I never really was a wine drinker anyway. I felt confident that I was free from the desire for alcohol because God had delivered me. I felt, once delivered, I would never desire it again. I was wrong, and when I took that sip of wine, I immediately felt the desire for alcohol. It was the intense desire that I had felt when I was an alcoholic. An incredible desire to drink again was burning in my soul, and that desire flooded me like a moth drawn to a flame.

I left their house immediately, and walked toward my house in fear, asking myself what I had just done. I asked the Lord for forgiveness and mercy and asked for His help. I was afraid of becoming an alcoholic again and didn't want to return to the road that I left long ago. I cannot describe the fear and anxiety I was feeling; I was almost in tears, remembering all of the pain I had caused my family when I was an alcoholic. Then the Lord gave me peace and took the desire from me. I know in my heart God wanted me to understand that I would never be able to drink alcohol again. I also realized that when God delivers you from something, you should never be foolish enough to return to it. I will be forever grateful for the things the Lord has delivered me from in my conversion: my desire for alcohol and the things that he continues to help me defeat with His grace. I won't test the Lord again, knowing that His grace is sufficient. I also now realize He was preparing me for what was to come, and my faith would be tested again.

Shortly after my experience at my neighbor's house, God allowed me to experience an incredible miracle in the Catholic church located in Connecticut. The church I was attending at the time decided to bring the Blood of Christ back to the Mass. Prior to that, there had been a fear of a flu epidemic in the area, and the church decided not to distribute the Blood of Christ for a period of time. One Saturday afternoon, right before Mass started, there were four Eucharistic ministers, one lector, a nun, and a priest in the sacristy. The priest looked around at all of us and asked, "Who would like to distribute the Blood of Christ to the parishioners?" I felt such a joy to do so, so I said, "I will." The nun looked at me and said, "Oh no, you can't!" I realize she said that because she knew I was an alcoholic and knew I would have to consume what was left in the chalice. She was only watching out for me. Part of me was saddened by her disbelief in the Real Presence of Jesus in the Blood. I have come to believe because of my past experiences with the Eucharist, and now it was time to experience Christ's Real Presence in the Blood. I looked at her and said, "I believe in transubstantiation." The priest gave me the chalice and said, "Whatever is left you must consume." I thought nothing of it because I was expecting nothing to be left, thinking that everyone would consume the contents in the chalice.

We left the sacristy with our orders and waited for the time to come when the Eucharistic ministers would go forward to distribute the Body and Blood of Jesus Christ. The time came and we walked forward to receive our chalices full of the Blood of Christ. I followed the Eucharistic minister who was carrying her chalice with the Eucharist, and I carried the precious Blood of Christ. We stood side-by-side, awaiting the arrival of the parishioners to receive the Body and Blood of Christ. There was one thing I didn't take into consideration: it was the first time the Blood of Christ was brought back to the Mass since the flu epidemic and, people still having a fear of the flu, wouldn't put their mouths on the chalice for fear of getting the flu. To my surprise, not one person consumed the Blood of Christ. I remember looking down at the chalice in my hands and was in shock because the chalice was full. It was now time to return the chalice back to the altar, empty. I went back to the sacristy where no one could see me and looked at the crucifix that hung in the church above the altar. I was feeling nervous and afraid because of my recent experience at my neighbors' house—I believe these two events happened within weeks of each other. All that was going through my mind in that moment was that horrible experience at my neighbors' house. It was still very much part of my memory.

I said to Jesus in the interior of my soul, "If this isn't true, Lord, I'm in trouble." In other words, if transubstantiation isn't real and the wine doesn't change, then I would be consuming a chalice full of alcohol. I consumed the whole vessel filled with the Blood of Christ and was totally shut down to my desire for alcohol. I could taste the fruit of the vine, but was unaffected. I felt no pulling towards alcohol; no addiction. This is a supernatural experience that I can't explain. Even today, I can consume the Blood of Christ at any Mass and never feel the desire for alcohol. God was showing me the Real Presence of Jesus in the Blood. To me, I can't deny the realities that I've experienced. It would be foolish for me to try to explain them to you; words aren't enough. Words in the natural state cannot explain the supernatural experiences. They can only give you a glimpse and a slight understanding of their realities.

Confession for the Forgiveness of Sins

I wasn't back in the Catholic Church for long, before I felt the desire to go to Confession. When I was with my Protestant brothers and sisters, they had been telling me, "All you have to do is to accept Jesus Christ as Lord and Savior and confess your sins to Him and you are forgiven." It appeared easy enough to do, but when I did it, I still felt incomplete. I didn't feel truly forgiven—I felt something was missing which I believe was grace. I was also struggling with much sin and spiritual pride because I lacked the graces necessary to overcome my sinfulness. I am not here to debate Protestant and Catholic teachings about Confession; I'm here to share my understanding and experiences through Confession. In my eleven years since my conversion I was blessed with two good spiritual priests who were also my confessors. I also had a period of time where I had no spiritual director because I felt the priests who replaced my first spiritual director in my parish were worldly and unable to offer me spiritual direction.

When I started writing the conversion, it hadn't been quite eleven years since my experience. I have had several confessors and I can sadly say there were times in my life where I felt my confessors were weak spiritually and very worldly. However, thankfully out of the six confessors I have had, only two of them troubled my soul while in Confession. In my opinion, they were worldly priests who struggled with pride and self-love. I don't say this in judgment, but in truth. Worldliness attracts itself to itself. In other words, worldly people are drawn to worldly priests and spiritual people are drawn to spiritual priests. None of us, however, can achieve perfection in the spiritual life because we all have a natural inclination toward worldliness. Not worldliness in the sense of materialism, but worldliness in the sense of our selfish nature. All of us will have moments in our lives where the self will surface—it's our human nature. But our strength is in Jesus Christ and all the intercessors we have in Heaven who can intercede for us.

So why do we go to Confession? Let me try to share my understanding, not in contradiction with the Church's teachings, but merging a different perspective of the same teaching. I found in my Protestant and Catholic brothers and sisters a certain kind of spiritual weakness. This weakness is the inability to achieve a deeper spiritual union with God. So what evidence do I have to support this thinking? Pride is the most destructive path for the soul. Remember God rejects arrogance, and Holy Scripture supports this thinking. Most of us don't realize it, but it's our pride that keeps us from going to Confession. We can make a thousand excuses for why we don't go, but the bottom line is, it's our pride. God loves the humble soul, and to achieve that deep intimacy with God we must humble ourselves before Him. It's through humility that you can receive graces necessary to overcome sin.

When we understand and accept our nothingness, we also realize we can do nothing without the help of God's grace. This doesn't mean we're helpless. We need to understand our dependency on God's grace and His mercy. In myself I can do nothing, and in Christ's I can do all things: that is true. So we need to accept our nothingness and the reality that in our own strength we will fail. Only in Christ's can I achieve great things. I can rise above the things that hold my soul to this fallen world. What about accountability for our sins? If I confess my sins while alone with Jesus and not to a confessor, am I truly forgiven? According to Protestant theology, I'm forgiven. What about my accountability to someone else regarding my sinful nature—is it necessary? The beauty about accountability is that someone else knows the misery of my soul. For me, this individual will be a

Catholic priest who may see me at Mass and know my struggles because my sins no longer remain hidden within me. The priest shouldn't look at me in judgment, but should look at me with a heart felt compassion. He should understand my struggles, my weaknesses, and pray that God will give me the graces necessary to overcome my sins. That's why it's awesome to have a priest who loves the Lord and not the world.

Dark secrets produce darkened souls. When we keep dark secrets, we're hiding something. Our secrets draw us closer to the picture we paint of ourselves, leaving us unable to see anything around us. The truth surrounds us, but we're unable to see it because we drew ourselves too close to the picture we painted. So, unconfessed sins are like dark secrets that can cause us pain. We bury them away in a secret place deep within us, thinking they're not harming anyone. But, remember, they're harming you—sometimes without your even having knowledge of it.

Even though we may not confess our sins to God, they still offend Him, thereby hurting the One we should love above all else. You can't hide anything from God. If you truly love someone, you find no joy in hurting them. True love can only feel the pain of what it has done when it offends or hurts another person. So why would it be different with God? It means that we're still too weak in our love for God, and think very little about how we offend Him. Let's not use God's mercy as an excuse to sin. We're abusing God's mercy because we're full of self-love. Is it possible that we try to justify our sinful nature in order to fit our needs and lifestyles? Sin in itself hurts! It doesn't bring joy to the soul, only to the flesh. The soul that truly loves God has no desire for sin. Even if that soul might struggle with certain sins, it finds no joy in sin. But the flesh finds joy in sin and doesn't see the harm it's causing itself. I find myself trying to see my own sinful nature and, with God's grace, He continues to open my eyes to how frail I am. Humility is the road to finding God. Pride is the road that walks away from God.

Spiritual Death and the Importance of a Soul's Decisions

I would like to talk about something which I call spiritual death that happened to me with two different confessors. I call it spiritual death for this reason: when I left the confessional, I felt worse than when I entered. How is this possible? Let me explain: worldly priests don't make great confessors unless you're a worldly person. As you grow in the love of God and the things of God, you grow in spirit. We know there are levels of spiritual union, and we should try to achieve the deepest union with God possible with the help of His grace. Saint Catherine of Siena best explained how this can be achieved. She said the soul is always in motion. I pondered that and tried to make more sense of it. If that is correct, then the world is at one end and God is at the other end. Let's start the individual in the middle. So, every decision that the soul makes is a movement. It doesn't remain in the same place as Saint Catherine tells us. Therefore, each decision a person makes either moves them toward God and away from the world, or toward the world and away from God. So over time, if the soul keeps making decisions toward the world, the soul embraces the world and will be unable to feel and embrace God's love. However, if it makes decisions toward God, the soul can embrace and feel God's love and move away from the love of worldly things. So it is for all of us here on this earth—there are no exceptions. Our decisions will move us toward God, or away from Him. The worldly priest in the confessional freely chose to make decisions toward the world and the things of the world. Over time, his decisions moved him further away from God, limiting his ability to embrace God's love. As a result of his decisions, he became spiritually crippled.

The first priest I experienced spiritual death with, finally left the priesthood and married a woman he was consulting. Let me describe this spiritual death. It was in a confessional booth where the priest and I were both separated by a wall with a screen that we could talk through. As I was confessing my sins, I felt as if my sins hit the wall of the confessional and fell to the ground at my feet—as if a wall of unforgiveness existed. Don't get me wrong—we still receive forgiveness, even if that priest is in a bad place. This experience was in a supernatural state. The best way to describe this is that I was trying to share my love with someone and my love was rejected. Imagine how that feels. In confession that day I felt empty, unable to feel God's love and forgiveness. My sins were falling on the ears of a man of God who didn't have the heart of God, but the heart of the world. When you love God truly, you love His people as well. When you love the world, you love the things of the world, not God's people. It will always be hard for me to describe exactly what I felt in the confessional that day.

Out of fairness to the priest and myself, I gave it a second chance on another occasion and had the same results. This happened to me twice with two different priests. I gave each priest two chances hoping it would be different: I can only describe it as a torment to my soul. As a result, I experienced periods of time when I didn't want to go to Confession, and this was difficult for my soul. I attended my church's annual confession until the day I met my new spiritual director and confessor which I believe was two or three years later. I have found through confession that I'm able to achieve a deeper intimacy with God and the frequency of my sins declines. I'm more aware of my sins and constantly ask God for the graces to overcome them. We'll always be sinners, but we should never accept our sins casually. We should always remember that sin offends and separates us from God, sometimes making it harder to feel his love. The mercy of God is great and words cannot describe His love for us, but God wants us to be free—not imprisoned by sin. We're slaves to sin and God doesn't want us to feel like slaves. We can find this freedom through the sacraments of Confession and the Eucharist.

Defeated by the Flesh and Breaking the Rules

While I was still at the Catholic church in Connecticut, I taught CCD for a couple of years. During my first year of CCD, I taught fourth grade with a women named Delilah whom I considered a friend. At first, we were very close and talked about our faith often. But true faith is not simply words. Words cannot sustain you through persecution and the desires of the flesh. Eventually, she yielded to the desires of her flesh. I really enjoyed Delilah's company because I thought she loved the Church and her faith, but I was wrong—she loved herself more than her beliefs. Most people will meet God on their terms and not His. They'll make God a god of convenience, fitting God into their lifestyle and not adjusting their lifestyle to meet the call of a true Christian.

I tried to help Delilah, through the understanding and the love of the Lord, and I also tried to help her let go of her desires of her flesh. For a little while, she seemed to be doing well, but the soul without grace is like a body without food.

In the fourth grade classroom where we taught, we were able to converse a lot about our faith as well as teach the students. My heart was not into teaching fourth graders because the energy inside my soul wanted to converse with adults. The Lord knew my heart, and in the following year I was asked to teach the eighth grade. Delilah remained in the fourth. We eventually grew apart and only talked on occasion from that point on.

I really enjoyed teaching the eighth grade because I was able to communicate with young adults and get them to question their thinking about God and their own lives. Also in the same year, I was a sponsor for a young girl who wished to be confirmed in the Catholic Church. She was in the RCIA program in Connecticut. The director of my parish religious education program (DRE) in Connecticut was also in charge of the CCD program and the RCIA program for another neighboring town. She was my supervisor, so if I had any questions about the CCD program, I would ask her for guidance or advice. While I was attending classes with the young girl in the RCIA program, I found out there were two couples—one from my parish and one from the neighboring parish—that were trying to receive certain sacraments. They were forbidden from receiving these sacraments from the Catholic Church because they were married and divorced and neither couple had received an annulment. At the same time, Delilah was sponsoring her husband who was going to receive sacraments, as well. Delilah became close friends with one of the couples from our church which put a strain on our friendship because I knew that the two couples couldn't receive sacraments in the Church and Delilah felt I should stay out of it. I always tell people the Lord puts you everywhere you don't want to be. I was put in a difficult predicament that would eventually cost me my reputation and everything I was in that church.

I approached the DRE about this dilemma. I told her that the Catholic Church forbids anyone who is divorced and remarried without receiving an annulment to receive a sacrament such as Confirmation or Baptism. She wasn't happy about my discovering what she was doing. She told me everything was okay and not to worry. I felt she wasn't telling me the truth, so I investigated and called the local chancery which administered the church I belonged to. I talked to the coordinator's supervisor and she informed me that the proper paperwork was not filled out. I felt in my heart it was all about the numbers and not the souls. It was like the DRE was recruiting people just so that she could secure her job. I approached her a second time with no success. Shortly after I approached her, she informed the pastor of what I was doing. I had to meet with the pastor and present him with documentation forbidding the two couples to receive any sacraments. In our conversation, he told me he had pastoral rights which overrode my documentation. I found this hard to believe, so the following day I called the monsignor at the chancery in Connecticut and he told me to talk to the canon lawyer for the diocese. I have to admit I was intimidated, thinking in my mind that I was an uneducated individual in the teachings of the Catholic Church.

Shortly after my conversation with the monsignor, I called the canon lawyer who agreed to talk with me about this dilemma. We conversed for a while and I felt I was at a disadvantage because of his knowledge, but in the end the Holy Spirit prevailed. At the end of our conversation, the lawyer said to me, "Mr. Saul, we don't know what went on in the confessional between the individual and the priest." I heard his words and waited for the prompting of the Holy Spirit to guide me. The response I received interiorly which I repeated to the lawyer was, "But we don't know if they'll meet the criteria of the annulment." His response was, "Mr. Saul, have a good day. Goodbye." the truth is, we don't know if they would have met the criteria of the annulment, and if they didn't meet the criteria, then they couldn't receive the sacraments according to Church teachings.

The thing that troubled me the most was that I was defending Catholic Church teachings and being persecuted by fellow Catholic leaders simply because I was defending the teachings. I wanted to be obedient to God and His Church and I always remember that the Lord had said to me before I returned to the Catholic Church, "Look past the failure of men and focus on the truth." So I try to look past the failure of men and focus on God's Church and His truth. I made a third and final attempt in the hope of changing the priest's and the DRE's minds, trying to stop what is forbidden by the Catholic Church.

In the meantime my wife and daughter had been allowed to come into the class so that they could be confirmed into the Catholic Church. Neither one of them had yet been confirmed. I have to admit I felt in my heart they did it for the wrong reasons—just to receive documentation—more for my daughter than my wife. I'm happy they were confirmed because I believe in the Sacraments and the power contained within them if you're a true believer.

A lot of things have changed since they received the Sacraments, and when I started writing this book, for example, my daughter wasn't married and my wife wasn't attending Mass with me weekly. I didn't want to rewrite certain parts of the book because, at the moment in time that I wrote them, those were the emotions I felt. I wanted to preserve them, so I decided not to rewrite them. My daughter Ruth did get married in the Catholic Church because I insisted she be married in the eyes of God and in a valid marriage. She agreed to get married in the Church because she knew how important it was to me, but unfortunately the sacraments she received didn't resound in her heart. This is a sad reality we face today—so many people receiving sacraments and walking away from the Church without embracing them. My wife, Mary, still holds on to some of her beliefs on spirituality and reincarnations, but is becoming more open-minded to the teachings of the Catholic Church.

I had been keeping all of my conversations confidential in order to preserve the privacy of those involved. Eventually, however, people in the class found out and began treating me differently. This next event troubles me so. In the final preparations before receiving their sacraments, the RCIA class had to attend a weekend retreat. The priest from my church who I had confronted regarding the annulment was the speaker. He said things about me which made me look foolish and embarrassed my family. In his mind, he felt that this subject was a gray area, regardless of what the Church's teachings were. He told the class about what we had discussed and his feelings about annulments. I was told by my wife, Mary, that after class a few of her classmates apologized to her and Ruth for the priest's actions, and told them that the priest should have never said what he did. My wife told me that the words he spoke made me look uneducated and foolish.

Some priests will try to form their own opinions, becoming disobedient to the Church and Its teachings. I'm not against priests, bishops, or religious educators forming their own opinions, as long as they do not publicly speak against the Church's truths. All of us have to make a decision regarding the Church's teachings. Many of us pick and choose what we wish to believe without truly investigating and trying to understand the meaning of the teaching, itself. I am also not naïve regarding corruption within the Church. Believe me, I hate it. I asked a priest friend of mine once to help me understand annulments. He looked at me and said, "Dave, in New York anyone can get an annulment, but in Africa very few can." I asked him, "Why is that?" He looked at me with a sad smile on his face and said, "In New York there is no shortage of money, but in Africa there is." Then he explained further to me how the system was corrupt, but he didn't speak against the Church's teachings. What he said troubled me because I didn't want to believe it, but I had to face the reality. In my opinion, he's a good priest. He didn't contradict the Church or Its teachings, but helped me understand human weaknesses which sometimes lead to corruption and scandal in the Church.

I would like to discuss another thing about the Church and all Its rules. In my journey, I have come across quite a few people who have complained to me about all of the Church's rules—which they call man-made rules. I have also found that a lot of people don't understand the Holy Spirit and how it inspires a person to think the way he or she does. I feel that without truly understanding the Holy Spirit, it would be pointless to try to explain the Church's rules and the thinking behind them. I can only tell you from my experience with the Spirit it doesn't think as a person would think, but it thinks in the mind of God in the hope of drawing mankind to Him.

I've had a few people tell me that Jesus wasn't about rules, but about love. I tell you that even love has rules and boundaries that cannot be broken. When I look at Holy Scriptures I don't see Jesus coming against rules directly, but the hypocrites who were breaking the rules. When I read the Old Testament, I see God establishing commandments and rules for the Israelites to follow. Nobody likes rules, but without them there would be chaos, disorder, and mankind would be lost forever. We would be savage beasts, taking and conquering, defeating the weak, living without morals and respect for those around us. We would eventually become weaker ourselves and succumb to the savage beast that we once were. Every rule or law has a reason for it. It's up to us to try to understand it.

Obedience to God and His Church Comes at a Price

The third attempt cost me much—I was dismissed from teaching eighth grade CCD, with only three weeks left to go, by the DRE with the approval of the pastor. I was happy for my wife and daughter who were confirmed along with the others but, still unable to change anything, I was disappointed: the two couples who should never have received any sacraments, received them anyway. I began to wonder why God's Church was disobedient to itself.

To make matters worse, we also had problems in the Catholic school system with a principal whose name was Herodias. Many parishioners of the church viewed her as a poor example of a Catholic. A lot of parishioners were complaining about her lifestyle. As leaders, we should lead by word and example, because people look to leaders to be an example. One day, I entered the school and went into Herodias' office to talk to her about this matter. I've known Herodias for years and was hoping to reach her. She was furious at what I had to say and rejected my words. She told me to leave, which I did. Shortly after our conversation, word came back to me that the Catholic organization she bartended for were saying bad things about me. It was just a matter of time before my name became dirt in the school and the church I was attending.

Shortly after, the priest removed me from my duties as lector and Eucharistic minister and asked me to leave the church in Connecticut to find another church. I did. My heart was broken. It plunged into the darkness of despair. I couldn't find anyone to comfort me; even the Lord seemed to be out of my reach. My soul was pierced, and the love I had for the Church was being poured out upon the ground. My emotions could no longer sustain my love for the Church. I could only rely on the wisdom that God gave me.

Everyone I knew and loved would no longer be part of my life. Delilah turned on me, along with the church leaders, religious educators, and the principal of the school. My name was ruined. I was considered an extremist who had gone overboard, and nothing could change the church and its leader's paths—they continued on the same path they were on. My concern for souls held no weight. The politics within the system were too strong for me to defeat or change. I was defeated by a falsehood and His truth stood outside the doors of the houses of his people who refused to open them. I was left standing alone, feeling angry with the Lord for what I just had gone through to defend His Church. In my heartache, as the tears ran down my face, I emptied myself as I continued to cry upon the Lord's shoulders. And, when there was nothing left to say but angry words, my final words to Him, spoken out of the last ounce of anger within me were, "I will never be a lector or a Eucharistic minister again for what You have put me through." In my heart, I couldn't understand how my love for the Church and God would yield such pain.

Afterwards, I told my friend who attended the Protestant church about what I had just gone through. He asked me to come back to the church he attended. I knew in the depth of my soul I couldn't. I told my friend of my past experiences with Jesus in the Eucharist and in the Blood. I also told him it would be impossible to deny those experiences. It would mean the rejection of Jesus in these species and I couldn't do that. I told him I would have to find another Catholic church and start all over again, which I did.

My heart was broken; words cannot describe the abandonment I felt within. I felt betrayed by my friends and the church I belonged to. My heart had to come to the reality of the corruption in the Church among some of its leaders and religious educators. None of us ever want to see corruption in the Church. We would like to think of it as holy. But men and women are frail and without God's grace they're too weak to lead people to God. God must be the center point of our lives and, if He is, our branches will be the things of God. I would be lying to you if I said some of our religious leaders and educators are not worldly. It's sad, but true. However that doesn't give us the right to walk away from God's Holy Church. We have to confront our religious brothers and sisters with God's love and His truth regardless of the cost.

We, too, must always continue our search for God. We can never become complacent, because if we do, we'll think we're there. Believe me, we're never there. We should examine our conscience daily, see our imperfections, and ask God for the graces necessary to overcome them. God is always willing to teach us and to help us grow spiritually if we let Him into our lives. I can honestly say that the sufferings I've experienced in my life after my conversion have helped me grow in my love for Jesus. I say "after my conversion" because before my conversion I had no real understanding of suffering and its benefits to my soul. In our moments of suffering, we may not find pleasure in the suffering, but after it passes we understand the need.

10

Letting Go of the Anger and Returning to God and His Will

I finally ended up in a Catholic church in Massachusetts. I attended seven a.m. Masses on Sunday mornings. Most of the time I would attend Mass by myself. I can't recall when my wife started attending Mass with me on a weekly basis. Several months had passed and some time in July or August the Holy Spirit began calling me back to be a lector and a Eucharistic minister. I was trying to fight the interior communication but it was welling up inside me with strength and conviction. No matter how hard I tried to ignore it, it kept coming back, tormenting me. The Spirit would not take "no" for an answer. The seven a.m. Mass had only two lectors and I had no idea that they were going to lose one of them in September of that year. I found out later from the parish secretary, who happens to be my sister-in-law, that at the same time the Spirit was prompting me, some of the parishioners were asking our pastor, Father John, to make an announcement in order to replace the lector who was leaving.

Father John had a lot of faith in the Lord and he knew that God would provide him with a lector. By the middle of August, I responded to the calling of the Holy Spirit and I called my sister-in-law to ask her if I could be a lector and a Eucharistic minister at the seven a.m. Mass. She said that she would talk to Father John and the scheduler about it. The transition was perfect and I started lectoring in September at the exact time the other lector left.

Some people would call this coincidence, and that's up to each of you. I say that God is more a part of our lives then we can understand or see. God is constantly trying to reveal himself to us in our lives, but we're not looking. If we don't look, how will we see Him working in our lives? I was drawn to Father John because he contained within his spirit a humble soul. My soul was still filled with arrogance and needed to understand humility. I always felt that God put people into my life in order for me to extract or understand the virtues I was lacking. The beauty of spending time with holy people is seeing and feeling their holiness. And, if you're open to the Holy Spirit, He will enable you to see and desire the spiritual gifts that these individuals possess.

I decided to ask Father John to be my confessor and spiritual director. He agreed to, and is still my spiritual director today. There are many other small miracles that have happened and will continue to happen in my life. I haven't recorded them all, but I've recorded the ones I think are the most important. It doesn't mean the rest are unimportant, I simply don't have the space to write them all down.

Over time, Father John was transferred to a Catholic church in the next town over. My heart was saddened, and I asked Father John if he thought I should change parishes. He advised me to remain where I was. It wasn't what I wanted to hear, but out of obedience to my spiritual director, I remained at the church I was attending.

11

Forgive Others as God Forgives You

While I was at my new church, I received news that my former DRE was in the hospital, unconscious and dying. I remembered the pain and heartache she had caused me, and in my interior the Lord was saying to me that I needed to forgive her. Part of me didn't want to forgive her because of all the pain. In the depth of my soul, I knew I had to forgive her so that we both could move on. I got into my car and drove to the hospital in Massachusetts. After asking the receptionist which room she was in, I headed there, battling my emotions and trying to suppress my anger so that I could truly forgive her. When I arrived at her room, I walked in and saw she was unconscious and unaware of my presence. I stood in the room looking at her with mixed feelings as old memories tugged at my soul. I knew what I had to do. As I leaned down towards her ear, I could feel her helplessness and realized that she was going to die. An emptiness filled me because I was uncertain if she ever truly knew or felt the love of God in the depth of her soul. There are many who go through the motions of our faith without truly embracing the beauty and peace hidden within. As I drew closer to her ear, I said to her, "I forgive you." I don't know if she heard my words. In that brief moment, I felt at peace and asked God to have mercy on her soul. None of us can know the state of the soul in that moment when death calls us. We can draw our own conclusions, which most of us do. In that brief moment, I also lost all awareness of the suffering she had caused me. All I know is, I didn't want her to die, and had concerns for her soul's final destination. I asked Jesus to be merciful. We don't know where or how God draws his lines regarding Heaven and Hell. All I know is God is justice and mercy and, because He is both, I try not to abuse His mercy and try to avoid sin because of His justice.

I found out a day or two later that the DRE had died. The person who caused me so much suffering was gone and I found no joy in her passing. I realize some people would because of their bitter hatred for a person which they may carry until the day they die. She was gone from this world forever. Her footprints were laid in the sands of this earth, waiting for the ocean's waters of time to wash them away. Soon they become a memory which will also fade away from the minds of those who knew her, never to return to this earth again. I pray that she might know and embrace God's love, hoping someday we will be together in Heaven as brother and sister in Christ.

12

God's Ways Remain a Mystery to Us

Sometime after her passing, the priest who was responsible for my being removed as a CCD instructor, lector, and Eucharistic minister left the priesthood. He was also the same priest who had told me to leave his parish and find another church. When he left the priesthood, he married a woman he was counseling who was struggling in her marriage. I saw him years later in Massachusetts. He appeared to be unhappy. I walked up to him, we talked a little, and, as we were talking, his wife came up to us. He introduced me to her, then we went our separate ways. Part of me felt sorry for him because he seemed unhappy and, as wrong as it is, part of me felt some kind of justice for my suffering. I am still saddened today because he formed his opinion of me by listening to the advice of the former DRE and others. He overlooked the passion that I had for the Church and my religious duties as if they held no value at all.

Herodias, who I consider partially responsible for my being removed from the church, sued for divorce when she discovered her husband was having an affair with the woman who ran the school cafeteria. Herodias was also known for having wild parties with excessive drinking. I had a friend who had attended some of these parties and he told me the parties got to the point of drunkenness where people were falling on top of each other. One of the people was the woman who ran the cafeteria. I'm very familiar with these kind of parties because in my past I participated in similar parties. In our drunkenness, we rely on our senses and not our thinking, leaving us unable to reason. Our senses respond to our desires, opening the doors to flirting, which in return opens the door to sexual desires and fantasies and closing the door to realities. Sin consumes our mind, heart, and soul. Fantasies become needs, needs become wants, and wants require fulfillment. Then the senses search until they're satisfied.

I often think and wonder about the three people who I feel were responsible for my being removed from the church in Connecticut. Was it coincidental, or was the hand of God at play? I don't know, and will never know here on this earth. Is it possible that God could have been showing me that the suffering these three individuals caused me would not go unpunished? Maybe. God's justice is so complex that the human mind cannot understand it, but it does exist. This world remains without answers, only questions, about the justice of God. Let faith be your only answer.

Prior to my conversion and in the early stages of my conversion, I lacked a deeper intimacy with Jesus, living in external joy found in intimacy with other people. I remained weak in the flesh, unable to control my desires, constantly feeding into them. So it is with many of us. I am not here to condemn the three individuals who caused me so much suffering. I now understand them, and their weaknesses, as I have come to know mine. I won't ever forget what happened to me when I was trying to defend the Church and its teachings, and I will always wonder why I had to go through what I went through. None of us will ever truly understand God and His ways: we can only trust.

Defending the Power of the Conversion

I find myself, these days, sharing the love of Jesus Christ and my conversion story with a lot of people. In my journey, I've had people say to me, "You could have gotten to that point where you were ready to quit alcohol." In other words, I could have quit on my own. I consider myself somewhat open-minded and try to understand their viewpoint. If on the day of my conversion the only thing that I was delivered from was alcohol, then the possibility exists that I could have done it on my own. But it wasn't. So when people say to me that I could've quit on my own, I respond to their reaction by saying, "Yes, I could have gotten to the point where I was ready to quit alcohol, but there's one dilemma." They ask, "What is that?" I say, "On the day of my conversion, I didn't ask God to take away softball, weightlifting, and my foul mouth. And because I had no awareness of wanting to lose those desires, how did I lose them?"

Most people understand why God silenced my mouth from foul language: if I am to profess Christ, what kind of strength would my profession be with a foul mouth. I know from my own experience that when some Christians talk to me using foul language, it doesn't appear to be genuine. I feel pure love speaks from a pure heart and a pure mouth. Impure love speaks from an impure heart and an impure mouth. So why did God deliver me from softball and weightlifting? As innocent as they may appear to you, they were the roots of my pride. God rejects pride. God knew that my pride would make it difficult for me to find Him and to know Him and love Him. He knew If I were to find Him in His depth, it would be through humility. If I continued playing softball and weightlifting, I know in my heart I would have struggled with pride and it would have been impossible for me to remain humble. Some people might try to dispute this thinking, and that's okay. I know my own weaknesses, they may not be yours, but they are mine. I have no regrets, nor do I miss the things that used to consume my life. I spend a lot of my time trying to engage in the things of God, hoping to grow interiorly with God and to draw people to Jesus Christ, our Lord and Savior. I know when I am engaging in worldly things such as model rocketry, yard work, or taking care of things that God has blessed me with, I always try to keep God a part of it, trying to feel His presence in everything I say and do. He's my best friend and I cherish His friendship and love.

14

Though You are Weak I will Make You Strong

Approximately six or seven years after my conversion, the Lord put upon my heart the idea to start writing. I was a little perplexed because the Lord was asking me, a person whose grammar skills are poor, to write. My penmanship is also horrible and I have no typing skills. So I asked the Lord interiorly, "How do you expect me to accomplish this?" Shortly after asking the Lord this question, I walked into the living room were my wife was watching t.v. and looked at the t.v. to see what she was watching. I couldn't believe my eyes. There on the television was a commercial for a speaking program for computers that types the words as you speak. I grabbed a pen and a piece of paper, wrote down the information, and called the company.

After receiving a CD in the mail that contained the speaking program, I installed it. Installing the program was easy, but learning the program was very difficult. I struggled trying to understand it, and got discouraged. I'm not much for computers either. I walked away for a little while, but the Lord kept hounding me. So after several attempts at working with the program, I eventually wrote my first writing called "The Within." I had one dilemma because I lacked grammatical skills: my writing needed serious editing. Prior to writing "The Within," I wrote a test paper that contained my own thoughts and opinions, in order to test the new program.

In the past, when I was dating, I would write some poetry. I feel that I have a gift to write with little effort on certain topics when I have some understanding of them. But when I wrote "The Within," it was different from my past writings with poetry. Out of nowhere, "The Within" entered my thoughts as if it were a command. Without understanding this command, I was moved to go to my computer and turn it on to my writing program. Once the program was booted up, I spoke the word "The Within." No sooner had I said that, when words began to pour out of my mouth without thought or understanding of them. They continued to flow like water down a river until the writing was complete. After reading the writing, I realized that it contained information that I didn't have knowledge of. I sat, amazed, because I felt the Holy Spirit using me as an instrument while at the same time teaching me. The Holy Spirit took my gift of writing and moved it into a supernatural state. In the natural state, writing requires thought and understanding of the subject, but in the supernatural state, with the Holy Spirit's guidance, the gift of writing is magnified and used without thought and complete understanding of the subject. The Spirit entered me and I became the writer and the student at the same time. God, in His mercy and love, poured out His graces upon me. This allowed me to write in the Spirit of the Lord so that I could communicate to others, as well as myself, on topics needed in the new age of thinkers, in the hope that all should be saved.

One day I asked a teacher friend that I knew from church to read the test writing and correct it. After reading the paper in front of me, he told me it was good and found no mistakes. I found this hard to believe because I knew in my heart this was impossible. I asked him again if he liked the paper and he assured me everything was fine. At first I was happy with his response, but soon realized that it was improbable that there were no mistakes. A sadness filled my soul, and fear and doubt soon followed. The truth is, many of us cannot be bothered with other people's problems or needs when there is no benefit to ourselves. How many of us fail in loving and helping our neighbors, family, or friends because it requires some of our precious time. How often do we tell others we're too busy because we're only thinking of our own agendas and our own needs.

As time went on, I asked a couple of other people to read my writing called, "The Within" and to edit it. I had no success. I became discouraged, and told my friend Anne about my experiences with these people and that I felt they couldn't be bothered with editing my writing. Anne, being a great friend with good English skills, told me that she would edit "The Within." Shortly after Anne corrected the writing, we made arrangements to meet and go over the writing. When we met and Anne passed me the writing to look at, I have to admit I was shocked by the number of mistakes I had made: I was expecting a couple of mistakes, not a page full. Anne and I met on several occasions, as we continued going back-and-forth with the paper, until it was grammatically correct.

Go Out and Preach the Good News

After we finished the paper, I began to wonder what I was going to do with it. I was not moved by the Holy Spirit to do anything at that point, so the paper stayed on my desk for a little while. Shortly after, I wrote another paper called "The Lost" and gave it to Anne to be edited. We continued going back-and-forth with the writing until it was completed. Even today, as I continue to write, Anne continues to edit the writings, and we continue the process until we're both satisfied. Eventually, the Holy Spirit moved me to start distributing my writings. I started sharing them with other people and I continue to share them today. Some of the people I share them with also make copies and distribute them to others. We're hoping to reach other people, in the attempt to draw them closer to God.

The Lord again spoke to the interior of my soul and wanted the writings translated into Spanish. I didn't know what to do—I didn't know anyone who spoke Spanish. One day after Mass, there was a function in the parish hall downstairs: a benefit of some kind. I was the lector at the five o'clock Mass and, on occasion, someone will walk up to me and say that you did a nice job. When I was downstairs standing around with a coffee in my hand and looking around, an Hispanic woman, whom I didn't know, came up to me and told me that I did a nice job lectoring. I thanked her, we talked for a brief moment, and then went our separate ways. As she was walking away, the Lord spoke interiorly to me and said she would be the Spanish translator. I was filled with joy, and yet in that same moment I had my doubts. I was feeling unworthy and undereducated in theology and the Church's teachings, wondering if I might have been mistaken about everything I was doing. Sometimes it's hard emotionally when you have to face your limitations, surrounded by a world of intellects who look at you as if you were nothing and had nothing to offer them. Oh, how our pride turns us into foolish men and women, leaving us blinded to the things of God that are delivered to us by simple people.

After asking around, I found out the woman's name was Esther and she was the leader of the Spanish community in our church. I finally did locate Esther and asked her if she would translate the papers into Spanish for me. She said she would look at them and try to do that for me. I was excited by her response and my soul was filled with joy, because I felt things were progressing forward and God was arranging everything for me. Throughout my journey, I have found that when I've tried to make things happen they seem to fall apart, but when God arranges things, it all comes together.

I think a couple of months had passed when I was sitting in the chapel one day, feeling disappointed and wondering if Esther was going to translate the papers for me. I was having my doubts, as we all do from time-to-time. I had signed up for specific hours at the adoration chapel, and I was there during one of those hours. Inside the chapel there's a statue of the Blessed Mother which is located on the left side in the front. As I was sitting in the front, I looked at the statue as I often do when I'm saying my prayers. As I was reflecting on her beauty and meditating on the sacrifices she made by saying "yes" to God, I remember saying to her interiorly, "Mother, is this woman ever going to translate these papers into Spanish?" As I was waiting for her response, I battled my feelings as they continued going up and down like a roller coaster ride. I remembered the times that I felt the highs in the Lord and then the times when the world brought me down to the lows in my life. I was thinking how writing was hard enough for me, and now I felt more was expected. My journey seemed to be getting harder and more demanding. It was hard for me to stabilize my emotions and senses because I was still spiritually too weak.

Then the Blessed Mother spoke to my interior telling me, "You need to be patient, she will do this for you." Immediately after that communication, I felt at peace, knowing in my heart her words were truth. I thanked her from inside my soul, knowing she wouldn't let me down. Shortly after, I saw Esther. Esther told me that she had translated the papers for me. Immediately my soul was filled with joy, and I praised God, and thanked the Blessed Mother for her intercession.

Esther continues to translate and distribute the Spanish version of my writings. She's also part of a prison ministry and prayer group and has distributed the writings to many throughout the Spanish community and the prison. We've become close friends in the Lord and I cherish her friendship. Esther has been through a lot and knows suffering: she appears to me to be a woman with a lot of energy who tries to be obedient to God as best she can. Esther and my friend Anne have been a great inspiration to me and will continue to inspire me because of their love for the Lord. When I see people like Esther and Anne, I think of them as rivers flowing down from a mountain into the ocean that contains life, known as the ocean of God's mercy. This ocean that is filled with love, overflowing upon a dry earth in desperate need of Heavenly water.

Recently God has blessed me with an individual named Monica, who at one time, worked for a publishing house. She's taken all of the writings from the beginning and has re-edited them. She continues to edit the new writings as Anne and I finish them. I continue, and will continue, to write as the Spirit moves me. Anne and I will continue going back-and-forth correcting the writings. Monica, our professional editor, will continue to finalize them. Father John will continue to look at them to ensure there are no heresies or contradictions with the Church's teachings. Esther will continue to translate them into Spanish and we will distribute a new one every three months. This will go on as long as God wills it. And if God wills that the writings be put into a book for all to see, then praise be to God and to Him alone. Let it be known that we are all vessels that God uses to spread the good news of His love, and we rejoice in being part of God's plan of sharing His love which is intended for everyone. This very book that you are reading was accomplished with the help of Monica. Each page of the book has been looked over and edited at least three times, as Monica continues to help me revise it. I can't tell you the amount of hours that have gone into writing this book. There were times I just wanted to give up. There were many times that I actually complained to the Lord about writing it. He would always comfort me and put me back on track again. Finally, toward the middle of editing the book, He spoke to me interiorly and said, "If this book could save one soul, isn't it worth it?" I pondered on His words and asked myself, "What is the value of one soul?" The value is—eternal life.

We Are One in Christ

God has put beautiful people into my life and continues to put beautiful people into my life. Without them I never would have accomplished all of the things I've accomplished. God knows our limitations as well as our strengths. We must try to understand that we are all brothers and sisters in God's family and each one of us is blessed. Each one of us has a gift, or several gifts, necessary for building up the Body of Christ. No one alone is the Body. We can never take credit for our spiritual gifts, we can only give thanks and praise for them. I hope and pray that what I share on these pages will help you find our Lord and Savior in a deeper and more meaningful relationship. I pray that you will give thanks to our Lord and Savior for all the beautiful people he has put into your life. And, through your hardships and your joys, you will always give glory and praise to our God. I pray that you come to your nothingness, because through your nothingness you'll find your true self. Through your nothingness, you'll become a child who is totally dependent on our Heavenly Father. And, never look back to the world of materialism and sins for your comfort because it will only take you from Him.

We Are All God's Children

I ask that you learn from my conversion, because I was naked before the Lord and I never saw my nakedness. Not like Adam and Eve who were physically naked before the Lord. I was naked within by the clothing of deception. My soul was bare before the Lord and my sinfulness wasn't hidden from Him. The Lord saw my nakedness and clothed me with His spirit of truth. Then I saw my nakedness and I was ashamed. I saw my sinfulness and wanted to hide. The Lord saw my shame and, moved by His mercy, picked me up and bathed me in the pool of His love. He covered me with His love and now I walk in His love.

In our journey, every one of us must travel through the world of temptation, carrying the wisdom that God has given us. We must know our weaknesses and try walking in true humility, carrying the light of Christ as we walk through the world of darkness. We must keep our eyes wide open, knowing in our hearts the Devil is waiting for his moment to ensnare us in his web of lies that will lead us to everlasting death. Suffering knows no greater place than that place called Hell. Try to desire all that is good, despise that which is evil, and seek the truth. Then you can rest in God's love and His love will remain in you.

I was a child lost in the world. You called my name and I heard Your voice. You fed me spiritual food and drink. You educated me in Your ways. You sent me among wolves. You protected me, comforted me and carried me. If I were to say to You, "My Lord, thank you and I love You," it would never be enough. If I were to praise Your name day and night, I still would fall short of what You truly deserve. I give myself totally to You. I am but a small token—a small coin of no value—yet I know You will love and cherish me forever. To You, my Lord and my life, be the glory forever and ever!

Amen

Book 5

The Interior Writings

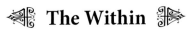 The Within

Oh Lord, I thought I knew You but I was wrong.
All these years I wandered never knowing.
I never really searched for You, but You were there.
I was surrounded by everything You created,
and I never saw You anywhere.
You surrounded me, and You were within me.
It took so long to find You,
and when I found You, deep within my soul,
I did not know how to love You.
You were very patient with me—
though I deserved nothing, You gave me all.
I was living outside myself,
never looking deep within myself.
You were always there, as You are with everyone.
You let me wander among the world.
You let me lose myself to the world.
You let me experience the emptiness of the world.
You still were deep within me,
You spoke from within me,
and I heard Your voice from within.
You poured Your grace upon me,
You opened the door inside, so I could come in from the outside.
So I left the world that surrounded me
and embraced You inside myself.
I found a new home inside myself with You;
the place where I can be alone with You.
The place no one can enter except You;
a place of silence, a place of peace.
When I go outside myself You are still within me,
and when I return You never close the door on me.
I know You are everywhere, and see everything,
but the best place to find You is within.

 The Lost

I have loved you from the beginning of time, and I always will.
These are the words I spoke to you before you came to be.
Know that I am in heaven always, waiting for you;
know that you can call upon My name at anytime and anywhere.
I was with you inside your mother's womb.
I was with you as a child when you used to pray to Me at night.
You were so innocent, so precious, so uncorrupted.
As you got older, we began to drift apart.
I watched you move away and it broke My heart.
You were searching for the stars, looking for happiness in all the wrong places—
you went in search of your dreams and left Me behind.
I tried to let you know I was there, but you never heard My voice.
You took the empty road, the road of sin, the road of separation.
I never stopped loving you, and I never will.
The sin consumed you, deceived you, and separated you from Me.
You thought you were happy, but the happiness only lasted a little while;
you felt so empty, so alone.
You cried out My name and never waited for a response.
I was there right by your side, but you could not see Me.
Your soul was so full of deception, it would not let Me in.
You closed the door to My face, and I stood outside.
I had so much mercy I wanted to give you, but
you never really sincerely wanted My mercy or My love.
So much I wanted to give you, so much you could receive;
in the end you were so lost, you could not find your way.
Lost and deceived you ended your life, how that saddened Me that day.
You never returned to Me for I waited for you.
You chose to reject My mercy and love for everything else.
I gave you free will and you abused it.
Now you stand before Me, broken, lost, and all alone.
I look in your eyes, I am saddened, heartbroken, wishing it could be different.
By your choices in life, desires of your heart, and your rejection of Me,
it comes to this. It hurts Me so much because we have to say goodbye forever.
I have loved you from the beginning of time, and I always will.

❧ My Last Day Prayer ☙

Lord, thank You for every blessing and every suffering,
for every person You put before me good or bad,
for all the days happy or sad, for always being there.
And if I should wake today, and tomorrow never comes,
let my day bring glory to You, O Lord.

Let the people I see today see Christ in me,
not like in the past, where I failed so many times before.
Let my day be an outpouring of Your love
for so many times I have hurt those You love.
Let my selfish nature remain inside
for so many times I thought of myself.
Let my personal feelings never get in the way of Your will
for so many times I did things my way not Yours.

Let me make no excuses for who I am;
I am a sinner in so much need of Your mercy.
Let me not justify my wrongdoings and shortcomings;
with Your grace help me to overcome them.
Let me be truthful to myself and others,
so I never deceive and lead others astray.

Let me desire what You desire;
it seems that my desires keep You away.
Let me have done all that You wanted me to do,
knowing there is nothing more You wanted me to do.
Lord, if today is my last day on this earth,
let my last words be words loving You.

Amen

 Alone

For those who can truly be alone with God, you will know,
understand, and never return back to the world.
God is the perfect lover of souls, the perfect friend,
the true source of peace, and the completion of life.
Before God came into my life, I walked a road searching.
I thought I had it all, not realizing I had nothing.
I thought I possessed it all, not realizing I possessed nothing.
I always wanted, but never really felt satisfied.
I was continuously searching and never found true peace.
I thought the world had much to offer, but I was wrong!
I fell into worldly addictions without knowing, and it imprisoned my soul.
Soon the light within me was almost gone.
Darkness filled my soul, it left me so alone.
I cried out to the heavens, my only source of hope,
and the hands of God opened full of mercy and compassion.
I began my new journey towards God and His love.
I left the world behind because I felt so incomplete.
As I grew deeper in union with God, the world seemed empty.
I could not find joy in those things that used to possess me.
The Lord tested my love for Him;
it seemed so hard I felt I could not go on.
At times, I could not feel the presence of God within myself
for God was going deeper inside me.
I was feeling empty, alone, with no desire to go back.
I could only go forward to the loving arms of God.
God was waiting for me to search for Him, to love Him,
to desire Him over all things in a perfect relationship.
A relationship uncorrupted without worldly desires,
from all the things that separated me from God.
You can build your kingdom here on this earth.
You can live in a world full of empty promises.
You can pretend you are really happy and continue searching.
Or you could begin your new journey towards God.
In the world alone, you will truly feel alone.
In the alone with God, you still can live in peace.
In the alone (the interior life) you will find God.
The world will always appear to offer you so much,
but only God will leave you feeling complete.

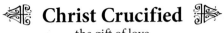

Christ Crucified
the gift of love

There are those who never heard of Jesus.
There are those who have and do not believe.
There are those who have and do not understand.
He left behind the greatest love story ever told.
For God was His father who sent His son.
Jesus came for the lost in the hope they would be found.
Jesus preached the message of His Father's love.
Jesus was also sent to die for the forgiveness of our sins.
Jesus performed many miracles, including raising of the dead
and healing the sick, spiritually and physically.
Jesus came as the ultimate sacrifice for humanity.
In the end, after all Jesus did, they crucified Him.
Did you ever look up at the cross and wonder?
Can you even understand the price paid?
The love it took, the pain endured, the sacrifice made?
What kind of love would suffer so much for so little in return?
For every drop of blood that fell to the ground
not one drop was for Himself, for selfishness never existed in Him.
This is the purest of love that denies itself totally.
Jesus never thought of His own needs, only ours.
So when you look upon that cross,
try to ponder the greatest love that ever existed;
follow the greatest example of love ever seen,
which Jesus showed us upon that cross.
The footsteps laid in the soil of the earth,
the ultimate sacrifice, the price paid in full.
The greatest gift of the perfect love.

(Reflection)

How Your heart must have broken when everyone You loved
turned and walked away from You and left You to die alone.
Only your mother, the apostle John, and a few of Your followers
were with You. The rest hid in fear or just forgot about You.
Most of the people there mocked and cursed You.
Why does such a great sacrifice not pierce our hearts fully?
Why do we give You so little in return?
Why are we too busy to spend more time with You?
Have we forgotten the greatest gift of the perfect love?

Shadows of the Soul

It sees but does not see.
It knows but does not understand.
It loves but loves nothing.
It wants and does not know what it wants.
It lives in a dream and finds no peace.
It searches and never finds.
It exists, not knowing why it exists.
These are the shadows of the soul.
We all want to feel loved,
yet sometimes we find it hard to love.
Do we put ourselves before others?
Do we ever look at ourselves for who we really are?
Does deception keep us from the truth?
Do we really care about the truth?
Deep within all of us exists the truth,
covered by deceptions of false dreams and images.
Shadows that deceive us from a deeper union with God.
All the joys of this world are temporary;
they cling to the flesh like drops of water.
In time they will dry up and disappear.
They form illusions blinding the soul from the truth.
They form a wall of deception deep within us,
creating a way of life pleasing to the flesh,
changing the true call of the soul to be in harmony with God.
Shadows are images or reflections—
but never are truly there, never real,
never genuine, and never to be held.

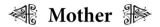 Mother

Where does one begin to describe you? For no words can.
Your yes to God, changed the future of the whole world.
Your loving heart brought salvation to a world in such need of it,
and the hardships you bore were for the love of God and all humanity.
You would not be just the Mother of one, but the Mother of all.
To those who never knew their mother.
To those who did, but never felt love.
To those who do know their mother and feel loved.
To the whole human race, know this, Mary is Mother of all!
How can words describe the sacrifices you made?
How can we understand the joy you felt carrying the Son of God,
and the crosses you bore for the rejection of your Son Jesus?
For the world rejected God's gift—His Son and yours.
They took your Son Jesus and crucified Him,
and you humbled yourself to the world that took Him from you.
Not one word of hatred or anger ever came from your mouth,
for you loved and forgave the ones who condemned your Son.
You trusted God totally with no terms and no conditions.
You carried the pain of true love and never complained once.
You shared in the joy of Jesus' resurrection,
and when your Son ascended to heaven you remained behind.
You continued the work of your Son until the day of your Assumption.
And from heaven, you continued the work of your Son.
For your Son was, and is, the hope and salvation of this world.
He said He would not return until the end of times.
You continue to appear to this world in such need of your Son.
You have come to us in apparitions and visions.
For you love the world, as God and your Son love the world.
Mary, our Mother, who loves each and every one of us with
a love so powerful that it cannot be described or duplicated.
For no mind could ever understand or conceive this kind of love.
Knowing this, let our thanks, as weak as it is, be some sign of gratitude,
to the Mother who gave all for the love of all. Amen.

Gratitude

Gratitude remembers even the smallest of things,
no matter how slight or insignificant the gift seems to be.
It remembers the giver of the gifts as well,
even if the person is just a small part of our life.
True gratitude should remember the giver of life.
Yet it seems at times we forget. Why do we forget?
Does our selfish nature keep us from remembering
to be thankful to God who thinks of us always?
Not just for the gifts He gives us, but because He loves us.
Are we thankful for every moment in our lives?
The laughter, the tears, the joys, and the sorrows.
Whatever it is in our lives You gave to us, Lord.
It is You who formed us through all these things.
It is You because You love us unconditionally.
You brought us into existence.
So let us see and understand this, O Lord.
Allow us to be forever grateful to You,
lover of all souls, to You be the glory forever.
For the days and nights long or short, You were there.
So much has not been said, so much has been forgotten.
So much to be thankful for and not a word ever spoken.
So many gifts we received, never to be given a thought.
Forgive us for what we take, and have taken for granted.
Sometimes do we think we work hard for things and deserve them?
Without You Lord, how could we ever accomplish anything?
How could we ever love? How could we ever care? How could we ever be?
We know we have forgotten a lot of these things.
Through all the trials and hardships You were there.
Do we really appreciate God? Do we ever give Him a thought?
Who would understand, unless one knew You were forming them.
You are the giver of all these gifts.
May our selfish nature never deny the gratitude that is truly Yours,
and let Your unconditional love never be forgotten.

 The Cup of Worldliness

We all have, and will continue to, drink of this cup.
For I have drunk too much already.
Every drop is like a poison to my soul.
I wish never to open my mouth and receive another drop.
My veins overflow and I wish it would leave me.
Slowly, with the grace of God, my veins become purer.
My soul desires to drink of a better cup—the cup of life.
How I long for that day when my soul will be purer.
My heart will beat again with the love of God,
freed of worldly desires and selfishness.
My vision will be clearer, and I can behold the truth in its fullness.
My soul in this corrupted state longs to be free,
free of all the things that keep me from my true love.
For worldliness comes in many varieties and tastes—
so appealing to the flesh, so hard to resist.
You, Oh Lord, hold the cup, and are the cup of life.
Let me close my mouth to the cup of worldliness,
and open my mouth only to You, the cup of life.
Take my veins, open them up, let them drain upon this earth.
Empty them totally, so not one drop remains within me.
Pour into me Your cup, the cup of eternal life.
Fill my veins, so I can be made whole.
Let our hearts beat as one and our love flow together.
Let our thoughts unite, let me immerse into Your love.
Imprison me, so the world can never get me.
Lock the door to my soul and throw away the key.
I will wait as long as it will take You to do this.
Continue to form me into what You desire.
Strip me clean, teach me Your ways, and I will find You.
For that day I await the arms of love I will embrace.

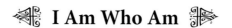 I Am Who Am

For no mind could even begin to understand Me.
For no eyes have ever seen Me, nor could they ever look at Me.
I let them hear My voice and feel My presence.
I allowed them to search for Me when I brought mankind into existence.
And I will allow them to continue their search for Me.
I gave them My commandments. I gave them ways to find Me.
I am, because I always was, and that is beyond human thought.
Who am, because I always will be. I was not created, I am beyond creation.
I exist within My creation. I exist outside of My creation.
I created everything that is, and everything that ever will be.
I created time and space, and everything within it.
I created every living creature and gave it purpose.
I am love in the purest form, if one could ever conceive that.
I am justice, **I am** mercy, **I am** forgiveness, **I am** love.
I created everything out of love with mankind in My thoughts.
I did not create evil. Evil came to be from a thought of the will.
Evil entered paradise, evil deceived man and woman
and man and woman became broken.
I allowed evil to walk the face of the earth because mankind chose to let evil in.
I never stripped mankind of paradise, it is still here waiting for them.
But they must choose which paradise they want—
the paradise I set aside for them which lasts forever,
or a temporary paradise here, which will lead to eternal damnation.
For inside every human being, I have put My spirit which dwells in everyone.
My arms are open, waiting to embrace them if they let themselves go.
I am who am, who will always be, I will never fade away.
But know, your life here is truly temporary, and your choice.
Know your choice will determine where you will spend the rest of your life.
Where do you really want to spend the rest of your life?
You can look to the heavens for Me, but know that **I am** here with you.
You can find Me. I am not far from you, you just have to open your eyes.
Look around you, you will see Me in all My creation.
Listen to My voice, you might hear it in the wind.
Listen to My prophets, through their voices you might come to know Me.
You are My children, will you return to Me? **I am who am**.

 Mommy

The voice of an unborn child :

Hello Mommy, it's me. I know we never had a chance to meet,
so many questions, and I have no answers.
I don't understand why you aborted me, please tell me why.
Mommy, help me to understand, because I don't understand.
You never gave me a chance, why didn't you give me a chance?
Did Daddy want me? How about you? Who didn't want me?
Did you think that I would have been a burden, so you had to let me go?
All I wanted was for you to love me, I would have loved to have been with you.
Mommy, I love you so much, it's hard to forget that day.
All I remember was hearing your heart beat and people talking.
They weren't very nice people, they did mean things to me,
Mommy, didn't you hear me crying for help?
Why didn't you help me Mommy, why didn't you help me?
I was crying in pain and it hurt so bad, I just wanted it to end,
Mommy, why did you let those people hurt me?
I thought you loved me, how could you have done that to me.
I remember I could no longer hear your heart beat,
I could no longer feel the warmth of your body, I felt so cold,
I could no longer hear anyone's voices, I felt so alone,
and then this Beautiful Lady appeared to me.
She seemed like an angel, and said she was my Mother,
she said she had many children, and we are all special to her.
I was no longer afraid or in any pain, I was happy again.
The Beautiful Lady loves me so much, and I love her.
She said for me to forgive you, and she helped me to understand.
Mommy, I forgive you, and I still love you,
I would like to have known you and spent time with you.
I cannot return to you there, but maybe you can come here with me.
The Beautiful Lady said for you to tell Jesus you are really sorry,
to pray always, go to church, and spend time with Jesus.
She said we would be together again for all eternity,
and Mommy, we would be so happy together.
I love you Mommy, I hope someday you will please come home.

 The Battle Within

Inside all of us, is a battle fought in the interior of ourselves.
This war is not fought with our hands or any part of our bodies,
the battle is against our human nature which includes our sinful nature.
Our will in Christ, against our own will of this world.
The love of God, against our sinful nature which offends God.
The sinful nature keep us from a deeper intimacy with God.
As oil and water can never mix with each other,
so it is with the sinful nature that is opposite of God, who is pure love.
God loves us unconditionally and gives us free will.
Does our will keep us from not knowing, not understanding,
and not accepting the very things of God and His love?
Are we too weak, too far from Him, to truly know and love Him?
Do we need God's help to remove certain sins that keep us from Him?
Does the sinful nature that dwells within us leave room for God to dwell in us?
Our sinful nature offends God, do we really understand this?
Our sinful nature makes it impossible to feel His presence and His love.
Unless we begin to search inside ourselves to find those things
that keep us from Him, we can never feel the depth of God's love.
There are depths to the sinful nature as well.
For example, the selfish nature—
Do you see love in the selfish nature? Can love dwell there?
How about pride—can you find humility there?
How about hate—can you find forgiveness there?
These are a few examples of the sinful nature which is opposite of God.
The stronger the sinful nature is in us, the further we drift from God's love
making it harder to feel His presence in us and His love for us.
If the sinful nature inside ourselves does not change, the circumstances
cannot change. Our emotions and how we treat others will remain the same.
With God's grace, we can rewrite the sinful nature inside us that is not of God.
God is love, anything opposite to that is not of God,
and if not of God, then it becomes a void within us.
These voids leave us empty and in search of something.
Unless they are filled with the things of God, you will be empty.
Why be empty? Fight the battle within, let God's love prevail.
From the beginning of time, remember what God called us to be.
We were all called to be the true children of God!

Fallen Houses

The Servant :

It saddens my heart that I have to write about fallen houses,
houses intended to bring mankind closer to God, Himself.
Houses fallen from within by the shepherds called to build them.
Prophets of God, fallen to this world, lost and drifted from the truth.
They have given up the things of God for the love of this world—
disillusioned and deceived, walking among the dead,
sacrificing their eternal life for the temporary joys of this world,
building kingdoms and paradises with false hopes and false dreams,
turning the sheep away by their very actions, abandoning God's sheep.
Not all of His shepherds, only some of the shepherds;
they were once shepherds of God, now shepherds of the world.
So now the sheep wander among the lost and confused,
looking to the shepherds for guidance in hope of finding the kingdom.
The shepherds cannot give a gift they do not possess, only what they
do possess. If they are worldly, they will teach the flock to be worldly;
if they are holy, they will teach the flock holiness.
The sheep do not need false hopes and false dreams,
they need guidance and protection from the shepherd.
So the sheep are scattered with nowhere to turn.
They see the shepherd corrupted and seduced by this world.
They keep searching for a shepherd to guide them to Jesus,
praying God will change the shepherd's heart and open his eyes,
waiting for the shepherd to return back to God and embrace His love.
For the houses are fallen and the flocks are scattered.
They justify their wrongdoing in the name of God.
This is not something new, it has happened too many times before!

Our Lord :

Tell the shepherds to open their hearts and minds to the truth,
to pick up their staffs, and return to the flocks to guide them to the gates.
Tell the shepherds that My houses are falling, and to rebuild them.
Tell the shepherds to imitate the life of My Son, to pick up their crosses,
and carry their crosses as Jesus, My Son, has asked them to.
For if those shepherds do not return to Me and My sheep,
they will have this world, and will receive no part of My kingdom.
So many have labored and sacrificed their lives for My houses.
Tell the good shepherds their sacrifices will not be in vain,
that their love for Me and My flock will not go unnoticed.
The gates of Heaven are wide open to the shepherds of My Son Jesus.
Tell the shepherds to bring the flock home with them for all eternity.

124

 Love

I ask you to embrace your most trusted friend,
for Love will never abandon those who embrace it.
Let Love rise above all things; let nothing come before it.
Let Love open the doors that cannot be opened
and close the doors that should never be opened.
I am not speaking of the world's thinking of what Love is
because it rewrites the truth of Love in a disordered way.
Love is not lustful or sinful; it is not perverted or corrupted.
It is pure, uncorrupted, and does not seek its own interests.
It is not self-seeking, but denies itself totally.
Love finds no joy in pleasing itself for it denies the selfish nature.
It endures hardships and suffering for the love of another.
It embraces the sorrows and the pains of those who suffer around it.
Love is the meaning of life. It is the tree of life with many branches.
Some of these branches are mercy, compassion, forgiveness,
truth, sacrifice, and friendship. You would be wise to embrace them, too.
These branches are almost as strong as the tree itself—
you can count on them; they will never let you down.
Love does not know itself, is not consumed with itself,
finds no satisfaction in itself—only in the joy of others.
Jesus showed us on the cross the true source of Love.
So I encourage you to look at the cross and try to understand.
Love will sacrifice its own life for the love of another.
It will withstand persecution, humiliation, and great pain;
endure suffering of all kinds for the love of others.
Beware of the enemies of Love.
You would be wise to never let them into the door of your heart.
Keep them in the back of your mind, for they will divide Love.
They are pride, jealousy, unforgiveness, selfishness, anger, gluttony, lust,
and the desire for power and wealth leading to the control of another—
any form of self-love that seeks its own interests.
They will only cause suffering between one another.
There is always hope in Love, and Love always offers hope.
You will find joy beyond your wildest dreams when you embrace Love
and Love in return will embrace you and never let you down.
Even if someone else's selfishness should break your heart,
never stop loving.
Love will always prevail, and you will prevail in it.

 Hope

Where does hope begin? Where does hope end?
It begins with God and should end in God.
Everything in the middle is part of the journey.
Sometimes we put our hope in the securities of this world.
Sometimes we put our hope in people.
Sometimes we put our hope in ourselves.
There are no guarantees when we put our hope in these things.
There is always hope through God when hope is understood.
When we put our hope in God and His will, then we can begin to understand.
We can accept what seemed to be hopeless and without meaning.
Although we will not be able to fully understand what God's will is for us,
we can know without a doubt: God knows what is best for us.
Remember the apostles, when they thought Jesus came to this earth
to establish a kingdom here, not knowing Jesus would be crucified.
They put their hope in the living Christ. When they crucified Him,
their spirits were crushed. Only after Jesus' resurrection from the dead,
and with the aid of the Holy Spirit, were the apostles converted.
Their hearts and minds were changed and they repented of their old ways.
They no longer misunderstood the focus of their hope.
Where do you find your hope? Where is the focus of your hope?
For us, hope can be found in repentance.
Through repentance comes the conversion of the soul.
For the soul can begin to unite itself with God.
It is so necessary for this to happen in order to understand hope.
Why do we put so much hope in so many things only to be let down?
Hope is a doorway that opens and closes by our will.
When the doorway is open, we feel the joy of our will.
When the doorway is closed, we feel the pain of our will.
One should never give up hope in anything or anyone.
Hope can open the door to many things—the possibilities are endless.
Try to understand—hope in mankind can only go so far.
Hope in God is endless and true in everything He created.
For if God created mankind and everything in the universe,
then surely He created everything for the love of us.
We hope because we love; because we love there is hope.
God is the purest love. God is the truest and greatest hope we have.
My hope is in my Lord and in His will, though I may not fully understand it.
I will trust in the One who loves me unconditionally.
And in that love for us, to hope in anything else would be futile.

 The Kingdom

Do not store up treasures for yourself upon this earth.
For where your treasures are will be the desires of your heart.
So why do we build our kingdoms here upon this earth?
Why do some desires possess us more than others?
At what price are our kingdoms built?
To those who wish to build kingdoms here upon this earth,
to those who have already built kingdoms here upon this earth,
what will be the spiritual cost?
How many souls will be lost for these temporary joys?
This worldly kingdom is a false illusion that deceives the soul.
There is no greater kingdom than the kingdom of God,
the cross that carried the weight of the world.
For what on this earth can carry that?
Let us not be deceived, for nothing here is truly ours.
We will hold on to the things of this world for a little while,
thinking we own them, and then we have to let them go.
For your kingdom here is truly temporary,
and your kingdom will fall into the hands of others.
Into their hands they will receive empty dreams,
false joys, illusions of hope, and temporary securities.
Jesus is the only treasure one should ever hope to possess.
His kingdom is the only kingdom that lasts forever.
So lay not upon this earth the desires of your heart.
Desire what is above and nothing short of that.
For in the faces of the angels and saints you will see
the joy they receive from union with their true love, God, Himself.
There are no false hopes, no false dreams, only the truth.
A kingdom built on truth. Truth alone. Nothing more, nothing less.
Life is temporary, so build upon the rock laid so long ago.
For many before us laid their lives upon that rock.
Upon that kingdom high above us all.
The kingdom that will never fall. That kingdom intended for us all.

 Mercy

Lord Jesus, help me to understand Your mercy.
My child, My mercy is easy to understand if you try.
My mercy is like an ocean with no end—
it overflows because it cannot be contained.
It is easy to access and yet sometimes hard to find.
If the soul is willing to believe in My abundant mercy
and truly believe, then the soul can begin to search for it.
However, if the soul does not truly believe in My mercy, it will never find it.
When people are thirsty, they search for water to quench their thirst.
So, too, must they desire to search to receive My mercy.
The ones who truly believe in My abundant mercy
beg for forgiveness because they are truly sorry for their sins.
They will receive My mercy and graces to help them overcome sin.
Sometimes I allow sinners to struggle with certain sins so they depend
more on Me, and less on themselves so that they remain humble.
They must embrace these hardships as part of My mercy.
They must come to the knowledge of their sinfulness,
and move past the deceptions in their lives.
They must search for the truth, and desire the truth.
My mercy is always there waiting for them to accept it.
Sometimes they refuse to accept My mercy because of their pride.
At times they are uncertain about their desires,
torn between their worldly desires and the things of Heaven.
They must choose heavenly things over worldly things.
I know the desires of their heart and soul.
So if you want to understand My mercy, then understand Me.
I am a God of justice and mercy. I am both.
Above all things, I am a God of love.
I formed man from the dust of the earth.
When sin entered the world, the flesh became weak.
It created the need for mercy to save humanity.
It created the need for justice for the souls that went astray.
I had to give My people My laws and precepts.
Some chose to disobey and they still disobey today.
A merciful God is a just God, and a just God is a merciful God.
For mankind is frail, free to make choices, good or bad.
Free to accept or reject My love, free to obey or disobey My laws.
Free to repent and ask for My mercy.
Free to reject My ways and receive My justice.
I am a God of love, and love is merciful and just.

The Wall

Jesus is the doorway that one must walk through to find God's peace.
We build walls right in front of the doorway.
There are those who build walls of glass.
There are those who build walls of stone.
They build walls right in front of the door that leads us to Jesus,
the only true peace they will have on this earth.
The glass wall allows us to see Jesus,
but prevents us from union with Him because of our will.
In our hearts we are sincere, but still too weak to let go.
We cannot seem to let go of the things of this world,
those very things that keep us from Him.
We try to possess these things and exist in both worlds.
The world of heavenly things; the world of earthly things.
We do not want to let go of one for the other.
When we divide our love, we minimize the benefits of our one true love.
So shatter the glass, walk through the door to your true love.
Jesus is our true love who is waiting for us.
When we build walls of stone, we cannot see the door to Jesus.
Our hearts cannot desire Jesus because we do not see Him beyond that wall.
So we live in the world, desiring things of the world, thinking we are happy.
We think that we are fine, not needing Jesus.
We think we know God, meeting Him on our terms, not His.
At least, through the wall of glass, we can see Jesus
and ask for the grace to unite with Him.
But the wall of stone forbids union with Jesus.
We stand deceived, unable to see beyond the stone wall.
We do not know the truth. We do not see the truth.
In that world there is nothing beyond the wall of stone,
no understanding of Jesus, no understanding of God's love.
Whatever wall we have built must come down,
for there is no wall that will allow us to pass through it.
It will always leave us standing on the other side forever,
unable to embrace God's love fully, unable to share in His peace.

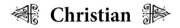 Christian

(A Deeper Understanding)

When I was gazing into the sky toward the heavens,
I felt the Lord looking down at me and I wondered what He felt and saw in me.
Then a thought came to me. Christian, what might you be?
So I pondered upon that word. What should a Christian be?
The word Christian begins with Christ,
which is the beginning of what a Christian is called to be:
an imitator of Christ. God is the origin of truth: Jesus is truth.
Christians have a love of God and love of neighbor.
They would not desire the things of the flesh, for that is the root of sin
which separates us from God. Sin keeps us from the truth.
Christians desire to live in Truth, which is God,
for outside of Truth are walls that keep us from God.
Christians see their own imperfections and do not accept them;
they strive for perfection in Christ through the grace of God.
Christians have a love for the Church.
Christ formed the Church. Christ is the Church.
The Church began through the apostles and by the grace of God.
The apostles led lives of poverty, charity, and selfless love.
They preached a message of repentance and conversion,
living in the truth of God, sharing His mercy and love for humanity.
True Christians live in Christ and Christ alone.
They do not seek their own benefits or needs in this world.
They live their lives desiring to do God's will, denying their own.
They live in the truth of God never misleading anyone for the love of God.
They would deny their own life for the love of another.
They desire intimacy with the one and only true love, God, Himself.
They still live in the world and love all that God created.
They see the beauty in the creation of God and accept it
with gratitude, reverence, and understanding of its purpose.
Never desiring it over the creator, Himself; always thankful to the giver.
I know I will never truly understand You, Lord,
and will always wonder if I am living a life pleasing to You—
waiting for You to whisper in my ear from above.
Will You call me Christian? Will You call me friend?

 Deceiver

Let us make no mistake; let us not be easily fooled by the deceiver.
He is very real and dwells among us,
looking for ways to keep us from the love of God.
He was there in the garden of Eden.
He caused the Fall of Mankind and our first sin against God.
That first separation from God and a life of paradise here on this earth.
But the deceiver was not happy—he wanted more, so much more.
He created more ways of tempting man to keep him from God.
He continues even today with more powerful ways than ever.
He sneaks in slowly, without our knowing he is dwelling within us.
He lets us think what we are doing is innocent and harmless to our soul—
then it's too late. Consuming us until we feel completely imprisoned.
Sometimes you cannot even see it, or feel it, or even know it.
God created us to be free and, in the spirit of the Lord, you are free.
Do you ever wonder about the things we love and desire in this world?
They seem innocent enough, seem to be harmless to the soul.
In time, we find we cannot live without these idols.
If we could only understand, if we could only see.
Whichever things of this world we intensely desire
will consume our thoughts, and we will elevate them above us.
Eventually, they will control us and we will become slaves to them;
they will own us, we cannot live without them, therefore we are not free.
It is the deceiver who keeps us from the truth.
It is the deceiver who keeps us from union with God.
We are like lambs lost in the wilderness too blind to see,
not knowing the wolf is getting nearer, awaiting to devour us.
The deceiver is the wolf after my soul, so it can be his for all eternity.
Keep a good watch in this world where the deceiver roams.
I was once lost. I want no longer to live with deception in my soul,
for these illusions kept me from my true love who is God alone.
To those who are too blind to see, to the souls who are misled:
You can find your way back. Look deep within yourself to who you really are.
Return back to God, and do not look back. Never look back.
For you know the deceiver's name is **Satan**.
He will not stop until you are his forever, damned in Hell for eternity.

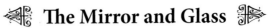 The Mirror and Glass

Lord Jesus, help me to understand and explain this illusion.
How can one even begin to understand these images?
From the sands of the earth comes the mirror and the glass.
For the glass allows us to see clearly through it.
When we stand in front of the glass, we can see the
things in front of us and the things outside of ourselves.
Some things are pleasing to the eyes, and others are not.
We see the things of this world, but are unable to see who we are.
And, when we stand in front of the mirror, we see the exterior of ourselves
and the things that are behind us, but we cannot see inside ourselves.
For the mirror only reflects back to us what is behind us.
We see the many things that we have accumulated over time—
some we will use and some will sit collecting dust.
We cannot see who we really are, only those things that surround us.
We see so many things in the mirror and through the glass.
We can choose to look at them, or not to look at them.
Lord we see these things in front of us and behind us,
but we never really look deep within ourselves for who we really are.
We are always looking to satisfy what is outside ourselves,
seeing through the glass and mirror that which deceives our soul.
If we only would close our eyes and look deep within ourselves to who we really
are. If we would look through the glass and see things for what they really are,
then look in the mirror at the images behind us as false illusions of joy,
we would no longer stand deceived by these images.
God created us unique and beautiful, called to be Love, itself.
Has time tarnished us inside, leaving us incomplete?
We cannot change who we are looking through the glass.
We cannot change who we are looking in the mirror.
We can change who we are when we look deep within ourselves,
and open the door inside ourselves to our Savior, Jesus Christ.
Let love pour into us and let God's love pour out of us.
So how will you live the rest of your life?
Will you stare through the glass and keep dreaming of things you might want?
Will you look in the mirror and hold onto those things behind you?
Or will you look deep within, cleansing yourself, making room for God?

 Table of Unforgiveness

Many sit at the table of unforgiveness, only to deprive themselves of
the benefits of love. To eat the food of empty lies and drink the cup
of bitter hate. I have sat at this table too many times.
How my soul has felt the pain of being unforgiving to others,
causing self-inflicted wounds because of my anger.
God did not intend for us to suffer in such a way.
We are not doing God's will when we refuse to forgive one another.
Why do we give in to our selfish nature? Is it because we are too proud?
It is hard to love those that cause us pain—their words seem to pierce our soul.
In time, unforgiveness separates us from those that God loves.
Jesus gave His life for all; there is no one on this earth excluded from that.
When I think of all that Jesus suffered for the love of mankind,
it seems too hard to grasp. Jesus forgave everyone who crucified Him,
yet we find it hard to forgive those who speak poorly about us.
Just words, and we disown them, sometimes never to speak to them again.
My heart breaks when I should know better and do not forgive others.
We are all called to imitate Jesus and to grow in love for others.
We should never have enemies because we are brothers and sisters in Christ.
If brothers and sisters in Christ, then we are friends of Christ,
and if friends of Christ, we are united together in Christ.
We are all frail, born into original sin, born into imperfection,
flawed by sin, and we continue to separate ourselves from God.
We continue to choose a life of sin when we sit at the table
of unforgiveness. Not just the table of unforgiveness,
but all the tables that the devil has set for us.
At these tables there are no plates that contain the love of God—only the plates
of selfishness, greed, pride, and everything other than the love of God.
So, join me as we leave our seats at the table of unforgiveness,
and walk toward the table of unconditional love and forgiveness,
where the plates overflow, and the soul never hungers.
Where we are the welcomed guests at the table of the greatest love.
In the presence of God Almighty, and all the saints of heaven.
Where the banquet never ends and the plates will never be empty.

Frail

What if we were able to stand in front of a mirror that would allow us to see who we really are? Would we be able to see past our exterior bodies, or is it possible we would be too blinded by the images we formed of ourselves, unable to see past our exterior body to the interior of our souls?
Does mankind stand, seduced by the world and all its empty promises?
Are we trying to satisfy our needs, attempting to please ourselves, but never able to do so? Always searching and never finding because we are empty inside.
Battling with pride, lustful hearts, and desires for worldly things.
Are we too blind to realize we are spiritually weak, trying to carry these desires that keep us from finding true joy in this world? These desires condemn us and are repulsive to our soul. One must be strong in God, first, Who is the ultimate and supreme ruler. If your strength is not in God, then the things of the world will tear you to pieces, leaving you empty.
For us, to rely on our own strength will not be enough.
For we are easily deceived by the things of the material world which weigh heavy on our souls, causing us to fall to our knees and to the ground we walk upon. Leaving us as frail as a stick trying to support a mountain.
The weight of the material world and its lies will crush us.
The world seduces the weak and weakens the mind to succumb to it.
Without God, we will fall hard and fast to the temptations of this world which are too strong for us to battle alone. The mind is overcome by the power of this world leaving man blinded, confused, empty and lost; unable to see the things of God and their true calling to love God and fellow man.
Who among you, if given power, wealth, and control of this world, would give it up for the love of Jesus, and live a life of poverty and humility?
I once lived a life seduced by this world and its lies.
I still struggle, but I do not struggle alone—I have Jesus Christ.
With the help of Jesus, I can now battle against the deceptions of this world, winning the battles daily, finding freedom and peace within myself.
I may never be famous, have power, or wealth.
I may never be popular, surrounded by so-called friends;
never travel the world, living my life chasing false dreams.
I will have my soul back, and to me that is all I really want.
My soul may never achieve perfection here on this earth—
none of us will. I will know and feel love again.
I will walk in the love of Jesus, and when I fall, He will lift me up.
I have something to look forward to that no one can take away from me;
I wait for the day to embrace Jesus, the true source of perfect love.

Father

Oh Heavenly Father, I know You love all of Your creation and always will.
I know You existed before time. You existed before Creation, itself.
In Your love for us, You created the heavens and the earth;
You created everything that is and ever will be because You are Love.
Humankind will never be able to understand You, though we try.
I, myself, wonder why You created us at all because You need nothing.
It is said You need nothing from us. I myself struggle with this Lord.
Is it wrong to say that our love for You, when it is true,
pleases You, and that You find joy when Your children show You love?
It is said that You created us because You love us,
and You created us in the image of Yourself.
Is it wrong of me to think that You created us, Your children,
because You love children? Even that thought seems hard to grasp.
We have no answers, probably never will, while here on earth; that is okay.
All I know is that You love us. Your love is the purest love,
but our love is impure, because our love for You is not true to You.
We have fallen in love with so many things of this world;
our love is divided because we choose to love so many other things.
Lord, You are constantly trying to reach us and we are too blind to see.
Throughout history, Your people have constantly let You down. However, there
have always been those faithful and devout ones who loved You so much.
I put myself among the weak ones knowing I could love You better than I do.
My prayers at times feel pointless; I wonder if they even reach the heavens.
My heart breaks because I am no different than any other person.
I know Your heart breaks too because You truly love everyone,
and would like us to love You in return—it is so little to ask of us.
We will suffer together, yet we will also suffer apart from each other.
I know my suffering helps form my soul so I can get closer to You,
but Your suffering is totally unnecessary and undeserving.
I know You are a just and merciful God who exists in perfect love;
Your justice and Your mercy are beyond our comprehension.
We are Your creation, created out of love, to love.
So in Your wisdom lies the fate of the whole human race.
Let no one be fooled—our ultimate end is in the hands of God.
Please do not abuse God's love; please do not abuse God's mercy.
Try to embrace God's love, and you will embrace Heaven for all eternity.

 The Cross

Innocent was the lamb, unblemished and without sin,
pure of heart, full of the love of God, obedient until death.
Jesus, our Lord and Savior, was born as the ultimate sacrifice,
to die for the salvation of many upon a wooden cross.
Jesus became the sacrifice offered up to God out of love for mankind.
God's own people turned their faces away from God's love by rejecting His only
Son, who was offered up as the sacrifice for our sins, beaten beyond recognition,
spit upon and disgraced, and left to die feeling completely alone.
Jesus even felt abandoned by His Heavenly Father, and in His last moments
before Jesus died on the cross, asked His Heavenly Father to forgive us.
Jesus did not die on the cross just to redeem us,
or to be the bridge to the heavenly Father—no He did not!
If that is all you want to see and are willing to accept,
you are missing out on so much more.
Jesus was showing us a life of sacrifice and love for us to imitate.
If we truly love Jesus, are we willing to die for Him?
Are we willing to sacrifice everything for Him; all our sufferings and joys?
Can we give up everything we own because we love Him?
Can we carry our crosses and unite our suffering to Jesus?
Will we be able to endure great suffering and humiliation for the love of Jesus?
Our suffering on this earth will be nothing, compared to what Jesus suffered.
Our love for others will never be enough in comparison to Jesus' love for us.
What about those days that seem to be so overwhelming?
We wonder if we can go on. You do not have to be alone. Look to the cross—
think of the weight of the sins that Jesus carried on the cross.
And, when people get mad at us, we find it hard to be silent.
Yet Jesus, "though He was harshly treated He submitted and
opened not His mouth," was silent. How hard that seems for us to do.
Jesus never did any wrong and surely did not deserve death.
He was totally innocent and full of love for the human race.
He was treated unjustly and suffered a horrible death.
None of us could ever be as innocent as Jesus was.
We will never love anyone as Jesus loves us.
None of us will ever carry a cross so heavy and so far as Jesus did.
What can we do with God's grace and God's mercy?
We can accept our crosses, which are our hardships and sufferings,
without complaining, knowing in our hearts it is because God loves us.
We must believe our crosses are for our spiritual benefit to help us get closer to
God. So embrace what is hard to love. Embrace your cross!

 Darkness

I know this place all too well, this place of darkness.
A place that once dwelt within me; it was an empty place.
I never knew of its presence until the day the Lord shined His light upon me.
I walked around in this world of darkness, living in darkness.
My soul did not even have knowledge of the darkness that dwelt within me.
Living day by day, doing the Devil's work without any knowledge of it,
living a life not pleasing to God, and thinking I was a good person.
Darkness deceives the soul, and the soul is blind to truth.
Darkness is the walking ground of the lost souls,
the home of the misled, deceived, and confused.
The blind walk around unknowing that the light is being extinguished
inside them, and the darkness gets stronger inside them.
They start to become heartless self-seekers, carrying out the works
of the evil one, and will have very little knowledge of sin or the existence of sin.
These people that dwell in darkness also form their own opinion of sin,
reject the Church's teachings, and accept false teachings.
They will live their life to what is pleasing to them and for their own gain.
When I walked in darkness, I had very little knowledge of God—
I had knowledge of God's existence, but that was not enough to sustain life.
Remember the Devil has knowledge of God's existence, too.
The Devil exists in total darkness and wants us to be there with him.
Darkness and light cannot dwell together at the same moment in time.
Nothing good comes from a soul that is full of darkness.
No one will be completely free of the darkness because we are all sinners.
Darkness is sin, and sin dwells in everyone. Love destroys the darkness,
love is stronger then sin—in your moments of love you cannot sin.
We have a choice: to try to be the light of Christ or to continue in darkness.
I have great strength in the light of Christ; darkness no longer owns me.
I am free to love in the light of Christ and not in my selfish love—
no longer lukewarm, but on fire, being consumed by the light of Jesus.
Happiness will be achieved to those who surrender to Jesus Christ.
Those who dwell in darkness do not know the true joy of life.
Darkness only causes pain to others as well as to yourself.
Light will always prevail, even if you have to die for the truth.
You will take that light that is within you to your new home in Heaven,
where you will be consumed and completely filled with the light of Christ.
You will never know darkness; it will never have power over you again.

 Fading Away

There was a time, long ago, when the prophets of God were true prophets. Men and woman who truly understood evil for what it really was, and still is today. Prophets who took a stand against evil for the love of God and the salvation of souls. They saw the destruction evil caused the soul. They understood God as a God of love, mercy, and justice. God spoke to His prophets, who in return spoke to God's people. They battled for truth, and died for truth, so that evil would not prevail, but there were many who refused to listen, causing them to fall away from God. God, out of love for His children, sent His only son, Jesus, to redeem the world and preach about His Father's kingdom. He was rejected, crucified, and died on a cross. The God of the Old Testament always blessed His children with much. Many took these blessings and misused them; it separated them from God. Jesus, in the New Testament, teaches everyone that we can have intimacy with God, through sacrifice, prayer, fasting, acts of mercy, and love. True prophets of God understand the meaning of the Old and the New Testaments—they do not use certain scriptures to fit their needs, attempting to meet God on their terms by twisting His words to accommodate their lifestyle. Jesus made a promise to send the Holy Spirit to give us supernatural power because man, being weak in his flesh, was unable to discern and battle evil. With the aid of the Holy Spirit, we can battle evil. Over time, evil has continued to seduce man so that many no longer desire the Holy Spirit. In time, the prophets of God slowly faded away. There are some prophets today, empowered by the Holy Spirit, still battling. The evil one appears to be gaining ground and has manipulated many to turn against God and His ways. He has deceived many, causing them to think they are equal to God, and do not need God or His church. They form their own perception of God to fit their lifestyle, resulting in the rise of false prophets, which is growing stronger every day. The true prophets are slowly fading away because the world continues to reject them. Their hearts are being crushed by the proud, disillusioned, and lost. False prophets will justify their wrongdoing, using Holy Scriptures to prove their thinking, taking certain verses from the Bible and using them to justify their lifestyle, setting a bad example to the lost and confused children of God.
This has misled many to think they do not need God's Church.
They no longer believe in sin, denying the existence and punishment for sin, choosing to believe and worship God in what is pleasing to them.
This results in the loss of intimacy with God and knowing the truth
They think God has equipped them with the power to create their own destiny.
No one can control their own destiny—it is in the hands of God alone.
Seek God in Truth, through God's prophets and His great saints. All the other prophets will bring you down the road of doom and destruction.

 Purge

May you never have to undergo the trial of letting go of the flesh.
It would be better never to have chosen the road of the flesh—
how much better I would have been if I had known Jesus growing up as a child.
Why did I not listen to my parents, grandparents, and teachers of the faith?
I could have grown in knowing the love of Jesus and His ways,
but I chose the world and all its empty lies instead of the truth.
Now I have to be purged, purged of every lie I have ever lived.
I choose to follow Christ now and must be stripped of who I am.
The world and the people I love seem to be left behind.
My way of life, understanding, and everything about me belongs to Christ.
I am rejected by my loved ones at times; they do not seem to understand.
I feel like I am being ripped to pieces. I now know sin is my enemy.
I am torn between the desires of the flesh and knowing the truth.
Unable to return to my former life and letting go of everything I was,
I am being crucified in my flesh. It is a pain that cannot be described.
At times I feel alone, abandoned and rejected by those I love,
sometimes watching the world walk away from our Lord and Savior, Jesus.
I think how Your heart must be breaking, Lord, because we are too blind to see.
I remember sin used to bring me joy. Now it only brings me pain.
Now I am being purged. My flesh is being crucified, as it should be.
The world is no longer my focus. My life is no longer my own. I belong to You,
Jesus. This pain I suffer for the love of You will only be temporary.
My vision will no longer be clouded; I will be able to see again.
My Lord will continue to strengthen me so that I can carry this cross of mine.
My biggest regret is the pain that I have caused Jesus—which He did not
deserve—because of my decision to reject His sacrifice on the cross. For a lie.
My true joy awaits me in heaven when I leave this world purged of the lies,
knowing the truth, understanding that Jesus never stopped loving me and never
will. Jesus, who loves us, freely chose to give up His life to save mine.
He carried the weight of my sins upon His shoulders—upon His cross.
He laid His body on a wooden cross freely, with nails driven
through His hands and feet, because He loves me and the whole human race.
This act of love deserves nothing less than the crucifixion of my flesh!
The pains of this purging will be nothing in comparison to Your sacrifice on the
cross. I know I can never repay You.
My life is Yours, Lord; do with me what Thy will.

❧ Worlds Apart ❧

Forgive me Lord. I have walked upon the face of this earth in my own world upon which I built my paradise—in a world of dreams on a foundation that crumbled under my feet. You gave me free will. I was foolish with it. I did not seek the things of God; I went in search of the things of the world. I feel like a fool, who in my own ignorance went searching for gold and ended up in a dry empty desert without spiritual food or drink. A fool trying to draw life in a meaningless journey to nowhere in a world of empty promises, false hopes, images that lie to my soul, deceived from my true purpose of my life. You called me to be Love so that I could become Love, but I turned my face away from You and became self love. Then You whispered in my ear and I heard Your voice calling me from out of the darkness to Your most beautiful light. Your voice tore my world apart. You left me wondering in a confused state; I had to face the lies in my world that I worked so hard to build. All the people I loved and spent most of my time with no longer knew me. Everything I ever loved crumbled before my eyes because I fell in love with You. You turned my world upside down. All that I ever loved became less appealing, without purpose—these things could no longer bring me joy. I did not know how to love you, You wanted so much more—I felt it was more than I could give You. So You went out and tested my love for You, and You whispered inside me," Who do you love more?" I replied," I love You more. "So I left my world behind, in search of You, leaving behind everything I ever was in hopes of becoming: a new creation in You. I chose a world of rejection for the love of You. I lived in a world between Heaven and earth, and in this new world of mine I am still unable to walk through the gates of Heaven and embrace You. I cannot see Your beautiful face nor can I share in the rewards of the heavenly promises. I cannot be with all the angels and saints. I have to survive in Your Spirit and, at times, it does not seem to be enough. The materialistic world does not understand me, so I live in a world sometimes feeling empty and alone, without human affections or love. I have nowhere to turn where I can find peace or comfort in this world. Even my prayers feel like tears falling from my eyes on the ground below me. They are unable to reach you, so I fall to my knees only to hold my tears in my hands, hoping you will take them from me and answer them. Oh Lord, there are times I do not even feel Your love. All I have are Your words to draw my strength, to survive. Sometimes even Your words cannot pierce the emptiness I feel inside myself. So I close my eyes in hopes of awakening to the joy I feel when You are with me, thinking back on those moments that we shared in Your precious love, trying so hard not to forget that love we shared. You, Oh Lord, know how hard I have tried! We may be worlds apart now, however I know this is only temporary. Let me draw strength in Your Spirit and Your love for I will leave this world with no regrets; I will leave nothing behind that can keep me from You. My world and Your world will be one.

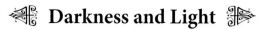 Darkness and Light

We are born into darkness and baptized into the light of God.
When we entered this world we inherited the sins of Adam and Eve.
We inherited the desire to sin, known as our fallen nature.
This nature we will battle the rest of our lives, against the world of
darkness, unaware of the damage it could be causing to our souls.
As children the small things we do seem to be harmless to the soul—
getting things our way, the small fights, and people spoiling us,
the things of the flesh—all appear innocent enough.
These are the things that began to form us into the world of darkness
and the world of darkness does not know true love which is God's light.
As we grew older, we freely chose to enter darkness or the light,
and if we are formed in the darkness at an early age, we will barely see the light.
The world today teaches us to love and please ourselves over all things.
We have grown without an understanding of what the true light is;
some of us even think that God's light is really within us.
So what is this light I talk about? God is the light which emits true and pure love.
This can be found in a pure heart filled with the love of God.
God loves the humble of heart and the humble can see the light.
The proud of heart dwell in the world of darkness, far away from the light.
The merciful, the charitable, the forgiving, are gentle of heart,
full of compassion, full of love, and full of the light of God.
The heartless, the selfish, the unforgiving, the merciless,
the takers, the greedy, the arrogant—all dwell in darkness.
Light and darkness can exist in the soul together, but only one will surface
at a time, which will be revealed by how we treat others at that point in time.
We must try, with God's mercy and grace, to exist in the total light
and to eliminate the darkness that dwells within our soul.
I know the world of darkness too well—it dwelt within me far too long.
Through the prayers of many and the mercy of God, the light entered into my
soul. I continue to search for the light of God which is truth and love.
We can continue to think we dwell in the light—believe me I thought I did.
We are not perfect because we are human—there will always be darkness
within us—and in those moments of darkness we will deny the light of God's love.
As we grow in the light, we see more of the darkness within ourselves,
our vision becomes clearer, and we see things through the light of God's eyes.
Let us move into humility, for there you can find the light and the truth.
You can move away from the darkness of your soul into the beautiful light;
you can share in the joy of the Lord here on this earth;
you can be the light of Jesus and shine in the world of darkness;
you can bring hope to a world in so much need of God's love.
So go out and shine—let the light of Jesus inside you radiate to the world!

⚜ Letting Go ⚜

Who among you can let go and truly desire Heaven?
Most feel the need to accomplish much here
and yet focus so little on getting ready for the next life.
You need to grow stronger in your relationship with Me.
I will prepare you for Heaven if you are willing to let go.
Do not be afraid; it is okay. I am really here, you just need to
believe—just let go of yourself from this world and all your desires.
Picture in your mind that you stand between Heaven and Hell;
that your life is hanging in the balance, based on your decisions—
the desires of your heart and your love for Me and My people.
Do you know that Hell is below you and Heaven is above you?
Envision that every decision you make is moving you closer,
closer to the place where you will spend the rest of your life.
Know that sin separates you from Me, it moves you away from Me.
Know that I am in Heaven trying to draw you closer to Me. Your sins offend Me;
they cause Me much suffering. In time your sins keep you from knowing Me.
Do you believe in your heart you are falling away from Heaven because of sin?
Have you ever thought of spending eternity in Hell?
Close your eyes, open your mind, and take a look below you.
All you will see is the suffering of many souls. Such great torment,
pain beyond human thought, and an eternity longing to be with Me.
Never to feel or embrace the depth of My pure love;
only the desires of the flesh and your sins that put you there.
Close your eyes, open your mind, and look above you.
You should begin to feel My love and want to begin to embrace it.
There is nothing in this world like it because it is not of this world.
My love is unending, and when the soul immerses itself into My love,
it will achieve ecstasy beyond human thought and emotion.
The joys of this world can never compare with the things of Heaven.
The desires you experience here will seem meaningless and empty
in comparison to Heaven. Is living a sinful life worth an eternity in Hell?
It will take time, sometimes a lifetime, to let go of your desires for this world.
You must keep trying. I know your heart and understand your weaknesses.
Fight the good fight, trust in Me, and you will make it to Heaven's door.
Always remember never to turn back, no matter how hard it may seem.
I will give you the grace. I will never abandon you. I will always be there.

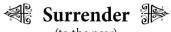

Surrender
(to the now)

You, Lord, are the lover of all souls and deserve more than what I give You.
For years I thought I could do everything without Your help—
I was wrong. I did not want to find You and I did not want Your help.
I was a proud man. A man of this world. A foolish man.
At the time, the world offered me so much, so I thought.
It seemed You had very little to offer. How blind I was.
I had all the answers and listened to no one; too proud to accept help.
Somehow Your light entered my miserable soul just enough
to go looking for You.
I continued my search for You, knowing Your love is always true;
Your love will never forsake me or abandon me.
You have blessed me with so much and will always continue to bless me.
Lord, for what little love I give You, You deserve so much more.
The decisions I have made in the past have separated me from You.
I submitted myself to the sins of this world which I freely embraced,
surrendering my will to the road that led my soul to
destruction—to a place far away from You, Oh Lord.
In Your stream of unending love, You poured love out upon my miserable soul.
You washed me clean, and let me bathe in Your pool of unending love.
I am not perfect. I will always be a sinner, constantly in need of Your protection,
always knowing Your love will carry me through the high and lows in my life.
So upon this paper, I confess my frailties and admit my weaknesses,
knowing I can do nothing without You, surrendering my will to Your will.
In this moment, I surrender my broken will to You, Lord.
How beautiful this surrender feels—my imperfect will uniting with Your perfect will.
Not as a slave to Your love, or imprisoned by Your love. No, Lord!
In my surrender, let it be a testimony of the freedom and joy I now have.
No longer a prisoner of this world, but a free man, a slave to Christ.
A prisoner of pure love, compassion, mercy, and forgiveness.
A testimony to my Lord, who saved me from the fires of Hell and a life of eternal
damnation. I deserved nothing and You gave me all.
I have the hope of someday spending eternity in Heaven with You.
Here I am frail and broken, deserving of nothing. **I surrender.**

Amen

 Death

The day will come when I will no longer awake—
never to open my eyes and see this world again.
The day will come for you, as well—for everyone.
I see death differently now, not like I did years ago.
Before I came to know Jesus and to grow in faith and love,
I was already dead and I did not even know it.
I was dead to Christ and the knowledge of his love for us—
too blinded by this world and what it appeared to offer.
By the mercy and love of Jesus, I live in a new life.
The words of Jesus have taught me to die to myself,
and live a new life in Jesus, and in Him alone.
My greatest fear is to deny my Lord and Savior, Jesus.
I asked for the grace never to deny my Lord under persecution,
and when Death is knocking at my door I will open it,
knowing that Jesus will be waiting for me on the other side.
I thought back when death would take me away from everything,
but now I know death will free me from everything here.
I do not look at Death as my enemy but as a welcomed friend.
There are certain individuals who look at death as the ultimate end,
who reject the things of God and His love for them; they think
there is no afterlife, no Heaven and no Hell. They believe it will be an
earthly end where their bodies are buried in the ground left to rot away.
It is sad, but true: their bodies will remain in the ground never to see the
resurrection of life, never to have their souls unite with their glorified
bodies. Their souls will leave their bodies behind forever.
God will pass His judgment on these poor souls who may end up in Hell,
and if they do, will live eternity in a life of torment, in true death.
Let the only death we fear be spending a lifetime in Hell.
May I spend the rest of my life doing the will of God,
so that when Death comes knocking at my door I will open it
as a welcomed friend. I will embrace my true love, Jesus.
I will no longer chase imperfect love, empty dreams, and false hopes.
Remember, if you are part of this world, Death will never be your friend;
but if you focus on Heaven, Death will be a welcomed friend.
You will be able to say, **"Oh Death, my friend, take me home to Jesus."**

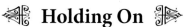

Holding On

Your ways of living life, O Lord, are far better than my understanding of life.
I am constantly searching, trying to understand how to live the life You want
me to live. My memories of the pleasures I once searched for now imprison
my soul, making it harder to let go of the desires of my past. They appear to be
part of me, and I want them to go away. My sins, which I welcomed without
knowledge, entered the house of my soul. I was blinded by these sins that
pierced my soul; they stayed with me, continually blinding and tormenting me.
I foolishly allowed sin to set up rooms in the house of my soul. Lord, I did not
know You when I allowed them into the house of my soul.
These unwelcomed guests do not want to leave—they want to take control of my
soul, and keep me from loving You and Your ways. I thought I was holding onto
them, only realizing they were holding onto me. We are entangled in a web
of right and wrong and need to be separated—one pulling on the other,
constantly tugging at my emotions and thoughts. The good versus the evil.
My body and soul wish I had never invited them into my life. These evil spirits
and their sinful ways torment my mind and soul at will without warning.
I find myself sometimes holding onto these spirits because my memory reminds
me of the pleasure they brought to my flesh. At times, I cannot separate the
things I have been holding onto from the things I need to let go.
I feel so foolish, Lord, because You have given me the wisdom and
understanding to discern the harm that sin causes my soul.
Yet my sin appears to be so appealing to my flesh that I desire it over pleasing
You. O Lord, in that moment when sin overtakes me, I think nothing of the hurt it
causes You. Satan's deception keeps me from seeing the truth.
Only after the sinful act, do I feel the pain of disappointment because I let You
down. I feel the guilt and sorrow because I offended You.
You O Lord, who are always searching my heart, as You search everyone's
heart, know me inside and out. You know if I desire Your ways or not. You know
if I truly desire to follow Your ways and precepts and live in Your truth.
I am weak, holding onto my sinful ways which battle against my desire to please
You. I lack the graces necessary to overcome my desires and weaknesses that cause
me to sin. You know in my heart and soul, if I could, I would never fail
You. How often I wanted to love You, Lord—I wish I had known You earlier in my
life. I wish the world never took me from Your loving arms. I will battle the lies of
my past, the demons and sins of long ago. With Your grace, I will fight against
the things I hold onto. I am a flower in need of watering—shower Your love upon
me. Let me grow in Your garden of love. Wash the dirt from my petals and make
me clean again. O Lord, let the only things I ever desire be pleasing to You.

 Time

None of us can escape time in this world for our life is in the hands of time.
God created time and the world we live in, a world moving in time.
Each one of us has received a cup—some a short cup, some a tall one.
We all drink of the cup of time and, when the last drop of time is gone,
our life goes with it. Some say it is not fair that they receive such a short cup.
Some feel their cup is too tall because of hardships and sufferings in their life.
Who am I to question the cup that God has given me to drink?
Some say time has no friends and waits for no one. This may be true, or is it?
Charity does not know time because charity does not watch time. Charity is love.
Because it loves, it moves through time unaware of itself moving.
Greed knows time all too well. It does not want to waste any time
because its fortune dwindles in every second that is lost.
The ones who know Jesus are not troubled by time or lack of time.
Their trust is in God and not in themselves; they do not rejoice in time,
nor do they fear time. They exist in time trusting in the Creator of Time.
But woe to the people of the world who live in fear of time running out.
They will spend the rest of their life trying to beat time. They never will!
They will fear everything that takes time from them: unexpected death,
diseases, and all the things that can take life away from them.
For some, when life on this earth is over, believe their bodies will remain in the
ground here on this earth, no longer existing because they think there is no
afterlife. Living their lives, bathing in the world of temporary joys, drinking their
time away, they are focused on things that will take them away from their
heavenly promise to the empty world below.
The true servant and good keeper of time will use it wisely to do the things
that the master has called them to do. They will wake every morning
thankful for another day and, when evening comes, they will give praise
for the blessings and the hardships that God allowed.
For when those who love God see their cup of life is running out,
they will not grumble or complain. They will praise God for every drop they
receive, understanding in their hearts and souls that the cup they receive
was poured out from a cup of love. This love hung upon a cross, and His blood
was shed for many so that death and time would no longer imprison them. They
knowing Jesus died for the forgiveness of our sins, giving us new hope in the
resurrection of life. Oh Time, my friend, I will not miss you if I make it through
Heaven's doors. I will no longer know you and you will no longer exist, for your
creator will no longer need you in this new world. I pray that I have used you well
in my life and, when the last drop touches my lips, we will say goodbye forever. I
thank you, my friend, for helping me reach Heaven's doors. Whether the cup was
short or tall, it did not really matter.

❧ Search My Heart ❧

O Lord, search my heart; You will not always find the true me by my actions.
Sometimes, my mouth speaks unkind words to Your children, and I know
that You love them so much. At times, I lack compassion for those You love.
I am not always a good example of what a Christian should be;
I am weak and have failed You so many times. More often than I should.
Often I feel like Judas, Your betrayer, when I am rejecting Your love.
How many times have You been there with me, and I turned my back on You?
How many times have I failed to profess Your name because I was afraid or
ashamed of You? Perhaps I was too concerned of what people would think of
me if I spoke about Your love for them, or how You died because You loved
them, or how their sins separate them from You, causing You so much pain.
My sins offend You! Deep in my heart I know this is true. Do I concern myself
enough to stop sinning and offending You? I just carry on like a careless lover
whose only concern is my own selfish needs and wants.
My soul suffers from the loss of Your love because I feel unworthy of it.
I travel through the dark night of my soul, feeling like a child abandoned by his
mother, crying out to the heavens and hearing no response.
My prayers bring no comfort, no consolation can be found.
Part of me is madly in love with You, while the other part of me is betraying You.
Without Your grace, I am nothing. Until I come to my nothingness, You will
receive even less of what I am—a miserable sinner drowning in his own sorrow.
When I come to my nothingness, I will totally rely on You, not myself.
You will become my strength, my fortress, the rock upon which I stand. I will
no longer stand alone in my weaknesses, but draw my strength from You.
Do not search my heart in my frailties and faults; You will not find me there.
Search my heart when I am feeling Your presence so strong inside me;
in that moment when You are my only love, and nothing else matters.
Search my heart when You are my everything and nothing can take Your place.
Not when I am letting You down because I am imperfect and lacking grace.
I know You already know that, but sometimes I just forget.
We think we know it all and have it all figured out—we are so wrong!
We let our pride get in the way of knowing the truth of who we really are.
I was afraid of facing the truth about my weaknesses—worried about what the
world would think of me—then I realized it did not matter. The only thing that
matters is what You think of me. What the world thinks of me will not save me.
Let what is in the depth of my heart be the only thing that You ever see.
Never look outside my heart, for part of me will always let You down.
Deep in my heart, I really do love You. I am sorry for all the pain I have caused
You and the pain I will cause You. My heart is Yours and will always be Yours,
even when everything else outside my heart is betraying You.

My Lord, You taught us to open our eyes so that we can see.
When I came into existence, I opened my eyes to this world,
too young to understand my real purpose in life, too innocent
to see and know evil. Unable to separate the darkness from light,
I was a child in the hands of the world waiting to be formed
like a leaf tossed around in the wind at the mercy and grips of the human race.
Potters molding me like clay in their image of what a person ought to be,
they were part of my life. I put my trust in them, not knowing God.
They had the power to show me the world of darkness and light,
teaching me to live in the ways of sin or the ways of the Church and truth.
I was raised in the love of God but never saw the world of light.
Even though my eyes were opened, I was blinded from seeing the truth.
The darkness in my life and my sinfulness kept me from seeing the light.
I walked and stumbled through life because I could not see the light.
Darkness surrounded me because I chose to let it in—it was so appealing to my
flesh—and what little light my soul could see was not enough to save me.
So my soul clung to what little light it had—a small dot of light in a body
consumed with darkness—unaware of the light of Jesus Christ, my Lord and
Savior. I plunged into the world of darkness. I felt so alone and incomplete.
My soul, in desperation, taking its last breath, cried out to the heavens.
The Light heard my words and poured out its mercy upon my miserable soul.
The heavens opened up and showered His light all over me.
It washed the darkness from my flesh which kept the Light from entering my soul.
The lungs of my soul were filled with the breath of life from the new Light.
The Light broke through the wall of darkness, and the Light flowed into my body
and into my eyes. I saw God's creation with new eyes and hope for a new life.
The beauty of the Light filled my heart and soul with joy and true peace.
I began to grow in strength and wisdom of the things of God and began to look
past the walls of darkness, seeing the truth that was hidden behind them.
I saw sin for what it really was and called to Heaven for graces to overcome sin.
I saw my selfish nature and the ugliness of my flesh and its desires.
With my new eyes, I saw the Truth and the Light. My flesh and soul became one
in union with the Light, no longer fighting against each other,
but working together as one in union with our Lord.
The Light is beautiful beyond description and our minds cannot understand.
I find the darkness is no longer appealing, but the darkness still torments me,
trying to win me back, always seducing my mind, in hopes of bringing me to the
underworld forever. My strength is in my love for the Light that allows me to
battle against the darkness. There can be no darkness where there is Light.
My eyes have seen the true beauty of the Light.
May I never turn back and see the world of darkness again.
Let those who have eyes see!

⚜ Pure of Heart ⚜

The Servant :

O Lord, hear my cry; let my words reach Your ears. Guide me; show me Your ways because Your love is true. I am afraid we might have forgotten how to love You, forgotten how to sacrifice, forgotten how to love others as ourselves. Are we corrupting our children because we give them everything of this world? Do we fail to teach them who You are and Your commandments? Can we ever love like children again? Is our childlike innocence lost forever? Tell me, Lord, what I must do to be pure of heart? I want to love You wholeheartedly. Do not hold Your words back from me; I need to hear them. Your words are merciful, just, and true. Spare me no judgment; I have failed you.

Our Lord :

A heart cannot be pure when it desires sinful things. You must fight against the very things that corrupt your heart—they only leave you bleeding in a pool of suffering, drowning in the misery of your own wretched soul. You will be discontent, constantly searching for Me, wondering why I am not listening—it is you who is not listening. You know the road to Me and still sway from Me because of your foolish passions and desires. Arise, O sleeper, from your bed of deception, and try harder to see the truth. What love on this earth can satisfy you and fill the voids of your heart? You wish to be pure of heart—only pure love can do this. Let go of your selfish desires and needs. Let go of your false hopes and dreams. Search for Me, and Me alone—nothing else will satisfy you. Do not pretend to be blind—you have eyes to see—open them. Let My light pierce your soul to the very core. Let it consume you in its entirety. Do not allow yourself to be half-hearted in receiving My light; be fully open to it. I love you enough to allow you to suffer. Through your suffering you will see the need for Me and rely on Me alone. Your empty love will be made full. Your pride allows you to act in an unkindly way towards others and harms your own soul. Your selfishness takes from others giving yourself more of what you do not need, leaving you more empty than before you began. Your anger does not only hurt others, but it hurts Me who dwells inside them. Your foolish desires never benefit anyone, not even yourself. To be the purest of heart you must dwell in the places where My love is, not wandering in places far from it. You can not drift back and forth in the world— try to remain in My light. Do not let the darkness pull you in. Let My love build walls around you to keep the enemy from harming and deceiving you. The Devil cannot live in a heart that loves. Always be open to receiving My grace. Desire nothing of this world. Accept and carry your cross. Seek the kingdom of heaven. Come to your nothingness and you will be filled with the things of Me. The purest of heart can only be found in the truest of love— nothing else will do.

 Walk With Me

My son, walk with Me, just a little further. You do not have far to go!
I know you are growing tired and your journey seems long—sometimes
even pointless. Open your heart just a little wider and trust in Me.
I was there when you turned your back on Me and left Me.
I never left you; I was right by your side though you could not feel Me.
I felt the emptiness in your heart and your soul.
I watched you walk through the forest, lost and confused.
I watched you walk through the desert, thirsting for water, unable to drink.
I watched you scratch the desert sand, but you could not find the living water.
You climbed the highest mountain and thought I was not there.
You sailed across the oceans, never finding what you where looking for.
You never found a place to rest, until you finally chose to rest in Me.
You never had a place to call home; now you know where to look.
I loved you enough to let you wander in the wilderness of this life.
I opened all the doors for you and watched you walk by them.
You grew tired of walking; you called out My name; I picked you up.
You asked Me, "Why did you wait so long to pick me up?"
I answered you, "Why did you wait so long to ask Me for help?"
I picked you up and dusted the dirt off you; I made you clean again.
You no longer walk in the world of darkness feeling all alone;
now you walk in My light. You will never feel alone—you will know **I Am**.
I did not say the road would be easy; it comes with much suffering.
There will be those who will persecute you and some will hate you and condemn
you. The world that rejected Me will reject you because of the love you have for
Me. My grace will give you life. My light will guide you on the road you walk.
Your enemies will cause you no harm. I will fill your mind with the wisdom of
Heaven. You will live in My peace and no one can take that from you.
Pick up your cross and follow in My footsteps on your road to Heaven.
Do not ever look back. There is no place you can return to. There is nowhere you
can call home. There is nowhere to rest your head. You have only Me.
Walk with Me, hand in hand, and together we will do great things. We will climb
the highest mountains. We will cross the oceans to the ends of the earth.
We will gaze at the stars together beyond the universe towards the heavens.
You will leave all your suffering behind that you carried for so long.
Your walk on this earth will seem like a blink of an eye. You can leave your cross
at the door; you will not be needing it anymore. The door will be open—come on
in. Walk with Me as we walk side by side for all eternity.

 Obstacles

In our unending search for the truth, we must pass through a series of obstacles. The truth is in front of us...behind us...the truth is all around us. The depth of our soul should want to desire to know the truth, which is God. In our journey which will eventually end in death, we must seriously consider whether we are truly searching for the truth in its entirety, or only partial truth. In this age of modern-day thinkers, many say truth is relative. If truth is relative, it would deny what truth really is, for truth must have an origin. It cannot be changed or modified, otherwise it no longer remains truth. It becomes a supposed truth. God is truth—He existed before time and space. Anything outside of the truth becomes an obstacle to freedom; not knowing or denying the truth becomes a great obstacle in our lives. It is said that we cannot find the truth, but the truth will find us. In our journey as we search to make sense of our lives, we try to understand our own existence and our purpose in life. We come up with more questions than answers. More walls than openings. Why does life seem so complicated? The truth is, we make our lives more complicated than they have to be. We are the ones who put the obstacles in our way. God created us to be free, not bound or imprisoned by anything, He does not put obstacles in front of us to slow us down, nor does He burden us with excessive weight. He is a God of love, not a God of slavery or imprisonment. So how do I find freedom in a world full of materialism, self-love, instant gratification, a need for power and wealth, and sins of all kinds? Freedom is found in God's love and nowhere else. His love does not imprison you. It does not control you. It does not own you. It does not possess you. If nothing can imprison God, then how can you be imprisoned by God's love? If God is free, you are free when you dwell in his love because you are part of Him. You are free to reject or accept His love, which means you are free to live in His love or to live outside of it: He never forces His love on anyone. The obstacles in our lives are put there by us when we live outside of God's love—when we choose to take control of our own lives and put God second. Only when you come to your nothingness and realize in your own strength you are nothing—only then, in Jesus, can you do all things. Everything you are is through Him, and Him, alone. I know we all want to feel like we are in control of our lives and our destiny, and to some degree that might be true. But eventually we have to believe God is in control of our lives or we will choose to believe in a so called truth, and believe in our hearts they are true, when they are really false. We have free will to make our own choices, but also free will to put obstacles in front of ourselves that will lead us down paths of hardship and unnecessary suffering. I am asking you to search your heart and soul; that is where you will find the doorway to the truth in its entirety. That is where God placed part of Himself—in your heart. He is waiting for you to open your heart to Him. Will you open up your heart to God and let the truth come into you?

❦ The Journey ❦

My journey began inside the womb of my mother where God's thoughts created me, and placed me with His hand in the channel of my mother's body. I lived and grew in a world surrounded by liquid and a thin wall inside my mother's womb, with a tube that sustained and nourished my body. I was not alone, Lord, You were with me and Your spirit was within me. My life depended on my mother's health and her safety; she was my lifeline. The day came for me to leave that world and enter a world unknown to me. I exited my mother's body into the hands of strangers. They cut the cord which sustained my life and slapped me, hoping to give me new life apart from my mother. I was too frail and needed the help of many to guide me and nourish me in this new environment. You were there, Lord, looking down upon me from the heavens. You never let me out of Your sight. Eventually, I became a man and the time came for me to move on. I sailed across an ocean of dreams, landed on the shores of illusion, in a land of promises which contained valleys and mountains which my emotions would respond to. In that place, I relied on my senses, allowing me to fall into sin. You were never part of my thoughts. I continually gave into my senses and my soul was conquered without knowledge—my soul was dying. I eventually climbed the mountain of sin. The higher I climbed, the darker it became and I was surrounded by darkness. One day while on this mountain, a light pierced through the darkness coming from the heavens. I saw my emptiness and decided to descend the mountain and walk across the desert of despair. From a distance I saw a well and headed for it; I heard a voice say, "Drink of the living water." I drank from it. The water gave me life. I turned back to see the world I left behind, which seemed obscure and far away. I knew I could not return to that place. I looked forward and saw many crosses on the ground along the side of the path. The path went up the mountain as far as I could see towards the heavens. Then the voice spoke to me and told me to walk along the path and pick up a cross and carry it until I reached the next cross. I was to put the cross down along the path and pick up another cross, and I was to keep doing this until I reached the top of the mountain. The voice said that these crosses would make me stronger, wiser, and appreciate the things I have been blessed with. The voice also said the crosses I carried would allow me to draw closer to His son, Jesus. His son carried the cross that bore the sins of the world. In this union, I would experience a great peace within me and live in the joy of the Lord. I would never desire to go back, there was nothing to return to. Every day is a new day with one purpose: to serve the Lord the best I can, without grumbling and complaining about the cross I have to carry. I understand it will make me stronger. Without it, I would fall back to the world I left so long ago. I walk with God by my side; sometimes He carries me when I am feeling weak, unable go on with my own strength. I try to follow His footsteps, avoiding as much as possible getting in front of Him. I try to trust in His guidance, knowing He knows what is best for me. In the end of this journey, I hope to spend a lifetime with all the angels and saints in a world existing in perfect harmony with our God.

 Castles

Most of us fail to see the enemy breaking through the walls of our exterior castle—our bodies—of which we are the keepers, meant to be kept pure and holy before God. Our souls are the interior castle which the Devil will try to enter and destroy. He must get past the exterior castle, first, through manipulation, causing us to sin. The Devil is shrewd and finds many ways to break through the exterior walls. He will try to deceive us through our senses because that is what we respond to the most. Sometimes our emotions interfere with the decisions we should make. We attempt to satisfy our senses without considering the damage it might cause in the weakening of our exterior walls, allowing the enemy to enter the interior of our souls. These walls will crumble without our knowing, and the Deceiver will enter the interior of our souls, destroying the castle from within. We must be vigilant in guarding the exterior walls, for it is through the desires of the flesh and sin that the Devil enters the interior of our souls.

We rely too much on satisfying and fulfilling the needs of our senses.

Our love for God is the fortress and the walls of the interior castle.

Our pride, selfishness, and instant gratification are the enemies to the interior castle. They will plant their roots at the outside walls in which they grow and expand, slowly and constantly penetrating the walls of the exterior castle.

We think that by satisfying our senses we have achieved happiness, and continue on that road without giving a thought to how it is damaging to us. Eventually, we lose the connection to God that is needed, causing us to fall deeper into sin and further away from God, upsetting the balance necessary to achieve a union with God. If this union is not achieved by the time the body and soul depart from each other in death, the soul might not reunite with the body in a glorified state in the resurrection of life, because the soul may be damned for all eternity. The interior life is your only hope of achieving true peace and union with God here on Earth. A strong interior castle can supply life to the exterior castle. The interior and exterior are one—body and soul. The stronger the interior life is, the stronger the flesh is able to resist sin. If the human heart, small in size, is properly maintained, it gives the body great strength and endurance throughout a lifetime. So it is with the interior life that glorifies God through our bodies. Conversely, a heart that is not taken care of properly, causes the body to become weakened, barely sustaining life, leaving the individual with physical suffering and emotional misery. The interior life, unattended, will lead our body into sin and separation from God, into a world of darkness. The Devil cannot pass through the walls unless you allow him; he cannot destroy your body until he has destroyed your heart and soul. The Devil will try to seduce the mind, knowing that by entering your mind he can destroy the exterior through sin and self-love. By penetrating the walls of the interior and destroying the love that dwells in the interior castle, he leaves the individual in a world of rubble and ashes, swept up by the winds of eternal damnation. The choice is yours.

⚜ Measurement of Love ⚜

If love could be measured by a cup, how would it be measured?
It would be measured by the size of the cup, the volume inside,
the purity of the substance, and the outpouring of the cup.
Each one of us has the capacity to love, depending on how much our love is
mixed with selfish love. The mixture of these different kinds of love exists in all
of us; there are no exceptions. We are all flawed because of our selfish love.
We all have different sized cups from which our love is poured.
Some cups are great in size: these contain works of charity, acts of mercy, and
unconditional and sacrificial love. Some cups appear to be small: these contain
just a few drops of unselfish love. The rest of the cup is filled with selfish love,
pride, and bitter hate. On this earth, we will never be able to hold a cup that will
contain pure love because our love is corrupted by our broken nature.
Do not be discouraged; we have hope, a source from which we can draw.
A source of pure, uncorrupted love with no end.
It flows from an ocean of love that is not contained or limited by anything.
The human mind cannot conceive nor understand this unlimited source of love.
We know in our hearts of its existence and that we need to desire to drink from
this cup of unending love. It is the only love that can help us to purify our love.
God's cup consists of many ingredients and its mixtures baffle the human mind.
It contains His unending love, His mercy, His justice, His anger, and His
suffering. This mixture which contains only love is not contaminated by a single
drop of selfish love. It is one-of-a-kind—there is nothing like it in the whole
universe. It can never be equaled or matched by anything or anyone.
It is hard for us to understand that in God's anger and justice we should feel
loved and know His actions are filled with unending love for you and me.
God's love is not measured by the same standards that we measure our love.
Our understanding of love is not true to the real meaning of love.
Our love contains emotions and feelings which are tainted by selfish love.
God's love is not tainted or corrupted by human feelings and emotions.
It is so important that we draw life and drink from the cup of His unending love.
If we continue trying to draw life from a cup that contains the poisons of this
world, we will die a slow death, breath by breath, until our bodies and souls reach
spiritual death. We will dry up and wither away, dead from spiritual dehydration.
The cup of darkness never allows you to see beyond the rim of the cup you
drink; its darkness and obscurity keeps you from seeing the truth and the depth
of God's love. The cup of life allows you to see beyond the rim and into its
depths, to which there is no end. His love is light, which allows you to see with
clearer eyes; the more you drink of this cup the more you see and understand
the truth. If you search the depth of your soul, it will thirst for this cup.
Drink up, it is free—you will not thirst anymore because this cup has no end.

Our Hearts

At one time in my life, I fell in love. Or at least with what I perceived to be love. Along with that type of love, came the responsibility of satisfying someone else's needs as well as satisfying my own. This love entailed responsibility and sacrifice which at times was difficult. We became one through marriage and yet remained very much individuals. I did not have a strong foundation in Jesus Christ, and what I thought was love was not truly love, but a love distorted by lust and self-love. I did not understand what true love was and it's true meaning. I perceived love to be what the world taught me it was supposed to be. My heart was unable to know what true love was until it became filled with God's love. My perception of love was to grow together, acquiring material things. My spouse and I had no concerns about the love of Christ, nor did we care. We only existed in the world's perception of love consisting of conquering others in the world, competing in a race against time, against each other for worldly possessions, notoriety, money, and power. We had no remorse or respect for one another. Everything became a trophy to place on our mantle. Over time, my heart became cold and insensitive; its only purpose was to satisfy my own needs. I did not care about anyone else's needs or successes. I became a conqueror and gloated about people's misery and suffering. Darkness filled my soul and my body plunged into sin. I felt no sorrow, no guilt, no remorse. I felt nothing—I was dead inside as my physical body maintained life. What can a heart tell you when it has no understanding of what true love is? It tells you everything and anything but the truth. It creates an image of what love is supposed to be. It misleads you down the road far away from true love. I know the emptiness and the heartbreak that comes with the love that is not true. I spent my life searching for love in materialism and the sinful things of this world, only to come up short. I was lost and blinded, totally naïve and ignorant to love. Our Lord and Savior saw me in such a pitiful state, His heart must have torn into two. But He never stopped loving me. Many were praying for me, and God heard their prayers. God answered them. God's love entered my heart and my eyes were opened. I was no longer blind and began to see through the eyes of love. I no longer spend time searching to satisfy my needs through things that brought me temporary joys, that only lasted for brief moments. No longer struggling, trying to satisfy my senses. I never felt satisfied. I was always thirsting, always searching, and never finding, always wanting. You do not have to spend a lifetime going down an empty road in search of love. All you have to do is open your hearts and ask for it. God's love is true, it is pure, it is unconditional without end.

⚜ Save Me ⚜

Words cannot describe the sorrow I feel in my soul because of the remnants of the sins that remain within me; the tormentors of my joy and peace in the Lord. Shadows and walls of darkness fill my soul with emptiness, leaving me feeling incomplete. False humility overshadowed by pride creates illusions that deceive my soul, leaving me unable to see who I really am, and who I am to be. Empty thoughts that never amount to anything, always falling short of my true calling, leave me unable to accomplish those things for the glory of God. Desire for things that leave me with temporary satisfaction, searching to fulfill my needs through avenues that are as temporary as the rest of my desires, leave me feeling upside down and paralyzed, trying to get back on my feet so that I can stand upright.

My perception is obscured for lack of light because of the darkness that surrounds my soul. Every sin, regardless of how small, blocks the light from entering the shell of my body and reaching my soul. The darkness affects the clarity of the vision ahead of me, leaving me walking around blind and stumbling across a path that contains the truth of who I am—who I am supposed to be. Oh, my Lord and Savior, hear my prayers and petitions as I stand before You. In such a wretched state, I walked around blind, unable to see who I am. I know I still have a long road ahead of me; I can only see the road as You continue to pour out Your graces upon me. Your grace is also the light that shines upon my soul, allowing me to look inward to the depths of my soul.

Your grace remains a mystery and without it we can accomplish nothing. There were many times I failed to ask You for Your grace. I thought I could do it on my own, and without it I would have remained in darkness forever. For years I closed the door on Your grace. I imprisoned my soul in a world far away from You in my house of sin surrounded by the darkness with the devil as my friend who shared his wonderful stories of how life was supposed to be. His words were filled with empty promises and lies, but he had a way about him that persuaded me to do many things. He was clever and created a world that seemed so appealing to my eyes which I could not resist, and he hid the truth from me. Then one day, You knocked at my door and Your light entered my room. I saw the devil for who he really was. I saw his lies and all the images he created within me. Lord, You saved me that day—I can never repay You. I need you Lord; I will always need You. The devil will not let go of me; he wants me all for himself. I spent many years in his company living a lifestyle of sin. The memories and the lies keep tormenting me, calling me back away from You, constantly calling me back to the world I am trying to leave behind. Lord, it is so hard when I know the truth. Forgive me; my heart keeps forgetting that You should be the most important part of my life. Will You keep showering Your graces upon me and save me, please save me?

 Arena

Over time, God's sorrow found its way into the depth of my soul leaving me in despair. The eyes of my soul saw with clarity the depth of sin in my own soul as well as the sinfulness in the world I live in. Words cannot describe the emptiness I felt—it broke my heart. With His grace, I have chosen the road that allows me to love God as much as is humanly possible. There are many in this world who have chosen to love the world over God; they have chosen to love the lesser of the two. I now walk in an arena, not in the physical sense. In this arena, I am persecuted because I have chosen to love God above all things. At one time, there were real arenas into which many devout Christians were dragged because of their love of God, sacrificing their own lives. I have been spared of that, but am persecuted by people's thoughts and words and sometimes hated because of my love of Christ. They refuse to hear my words or understand me. There are two other arenas in this world bigger than the arena I live in. The sports arenas of this world are the next largest with millions of spectators. Many attend these arenas and watch their gladiators play against each other for victory over each other. Some watch these events through man-made vessels which allow them to see their gladiators from the convenience of their own home. I call these playing fields, "arenas of glory." Many will sit back in drunken sinfulness, cheering their teams on while they scream and curse at the other gladiators. They let their emotions carry them away without a care in the world, and without realizing they drag themselves down to the world of self-indulgence as their senses begin to escalate and their souls begin to decline. The third arena is the greatest and biggest of them all. In this arena, God is the spectator looking down upon the earth at His children who inhabit it. Let us not forget that the eyes of heaven are gazing upon us. There is no one who can hide from heaven's view. How we act and what we do is seen from above. Millions of sins are seen from above while we try to conquer one another in the competition of life. Without remorse, we think nothing of sinning and offending God. Our sins are like arrows being shot into the heavens and piercing the heart of God himself. He loves us so much mere words are unable to describe this kind of love. The pain we cause Him is beyond description. Unfathomable amounts of souls in despair could not match the sorrow He feels. God's love deserves more than we can give Him; should we not make an effort to at least try? His hands are holding back all His tears. His hands are holding back the wrath of heaven that we deserve. There are some devout Christians in this arena; unfortunately there are fewer and fewer as time goes on. Will you enter the arena with a heart open to God's love, or will you stay behind and break His heart? There is plenty of room if you choose to join me. Will you join me in this arena and accept God's love?

 The Visitor

One night, when I was entering the depth of prayer, a visitor entered my thoughts and began to speak to me. The voice was soft spoken and contained a false sense of love—I was uncertain if it was my imagination or real.
The voice began speaking to me—"There is no heaven, there is no hell, it is all part of your imagination, it is all a lie. Why do you believe in such foolishness?" I answered the voice of my thoughts, "I do not know who you are...you are wrong!" The voice continued, "Why do you follow Jesus? What has He done for you? He ruined your life. Your good friends are gone. Many persecute and reject you. You are trying to be a Christian. Why would you waste your life for that? Do you know man made it all up? Why do you believe in such foolishness?" As he was speaking, a darkness surrounded me. I felt the cold of this darkness pierce my body to the depth of my bones, and my teeth began to chatter. I could not shake the cold from my body, so I crawled under the blankets of my bed. I uttered these words: "Jesus is my strength! Jesus is my strength! Jesus is my strength!" The voice responded, "You do not have enough faith to rebuke me; you are still a child with so much to learn." He continued to torment me with his words. He said, "Who are you in comparison to me? I have entered the thoughts of many, starting with your church. I have corrupted many men throughout history including popes, bishops, and priests. I have divided Christians, created false religious beliefs, and thousands of different denominations of believers who claim to know the truth. I have created false prophets and misled millions far from God's truth. I have taught many to hate, cheat, and steal, putting brother against brother. I am the cause of wars, I was there for numerous plagues, famines, disasters and diseases that resulted in millions of innocent lives lost. I am the master of destruction and death. You are nothing. I have reduced the truth and turned it into a lie. I created a world of nonbelievers, self seekers who are not interested in God and His church. "Again, I tried to rebuke him; I was afraid and doubt filled my soul. His voice turned to anger and he called me stupid. "I am Satan, ruler of this world! If you do not reject Jesus and return to the life you came from, I will make your life on this earth a living hell! I will turn your dreams into nightmares, your hope into despair, your peace into trouble. You will have no joy on this earth until the day you die. When you die, you will remain in the ground never to awaken again." In hesitation, I replied in return, "If what you are saying is true, then my new life in Jesus is a lie!" He replied, "Yes." I said, "No, because who I am and what I know denies what you say. My life in sin never brought me happiness, true happiness. I lived in moments and pockets of joy, never feeling complete. I also know what true love is, and the only person who can give me that love is God alone!" He replied, "You are such a fool! You will be rejected and hated by many. Even the church you love will reject you. Know this: I will torment you the rest of your life." The cold and the darkness left my body and soul upon Satan's departure. I know in my heart this is not the end of this encounter. I will trust in the Lord, my Rock and Savior.